CREATING A WORLD CLASS ORGANIZATION

THE PROFESSIONAL PAPERBACK SERIES

The *Professional Paperback Series*, new from Kogan Page, is a major series of practically focused business books aimed at professionals in the middle to senior management bracket. The series covers a wide range of leading edge business topics, including business strategy, organizational theory and design, leadership, marketing, project management and management style. This invaluable series is a mixture of new titles and new or revised editions of best-selling titles. For both practising managers and students of business, the *Professional Paperback Series* will give a boost to their skills and knowledge.

Titles currently available in the series are:

Commonsense Direct Marketing
Fourth edition
Drayton Bird

Transform Your Management Style!
How to Develop and Motivate Your Staff to Achieve Peak Performance
Hilary Walmsley

Total Leadership
How to Inspire and Motivate Through Effective Leadership
Jim Barrett

Designing Organizations
The Foundation for Excellence
Third edition
Philip Sadler

The Top Consultant
Developing Your Skills for Greater Effectiveness
Third edition
Calvert Markham

The Marketing Plan
A Practitioner's Guide
Second edition
John Westwood

Goal Directed Project Management
Second edition
E S Andersen, K V Grude and T Haug

Creating a World Class Organization
Ten Performance Measures of Business Success
Second edition
Bryan D Prescott

PROFESSIONAL
PAPERBACKS

CREATING A WORLD CLASS ORGANIZATION

TEN PERFORMANCE MEASURES OF BUSINESS SUCCESS

Bryan D Prescott

INSTITUTE OF DIRECTORS

KOGAN PAGE

LONDON, UK • NEW HAMPSHIRE, USA • NEW DELHI, INDIA

YOURS TO HAVE AND TO HOLD
BUT NOT TO COPY

First published in 1995
Second edition published as part of the Professional Paperbacks series in 1998

Kogan Page Limited   Kogan Page Limited
120 Pentonville Road   163 Central Avenue, Suite 4
London   Dover, NH 03820
N1 9JN   USA

The Institute of Directors accepts no responsibility for the opinions expressed by the author of this publication. Readers should consult their advisors before acting on any of the issues raised.

British Library Cataloguing in Publication Data
A CIP record for this book is available from the British Library.
ISBN 0 7494 2583 0

Typeset by Kogan Page
Printed and bound in Great Britain by Clays Ltd, St Ives plc

Contents

Foreword

In the face of fierce competition companies worldwide are becoming more customer orientated and in recent years many of them have introduced customer-centred initiatives. However, there is considerable evidence to show that the actual benefits of a customer-centred strategy often fail to match expectations. In my experience, this is usually the result of inappropriate leadership styles, poor management and development of people, and a failure to measure and improve the right things at the right time.

All too often management exhort employees to get things right first time, to operate effectively in performance improvement teams and to participate in a never-ending search for excellence. Yet, at the same time, they often fail to provide the training, tools, information and empowerment required to achieve these aims. All too often, enthusiastic and highly motivated people at lower levels in the organization drive improvement programmes forward initially, only to see the programmes lose credibility and momentum when cynical employees realize that senior management are paying 'lip service' to them. Unfortunately, there are far too many chief executives and managers trying to create organizations for the twenty-first century who still employ leadership styles more suited to the early twentieth century.

Measurement systems often measure the wrong things or measure the right things at the wrong time. There is little point, for example, in measuring quality at the end of a process when it is too late to correct faults or errors. Measurements should be integrated at business, companywide and operational levels so that people know what is important to measure and when and where measurements should take place – for example, on the process and as close as possible to the causes of faults so that preventative action can be quickly taken.

This book identifies ten performance measures of business success that characterize world class organizations (WCOs), and the performance improvement criteria underpinning each of the ten measures. The primary aim of WCOs is to satisfy the needs and expectations of their customers and stakeholders – ie their investors, their employees and the community, which is concerned about safety, pollution and ethical issues.

Detailing the management of change required to become a world class organization, the book illustrates how the ten performance measures of business success, self assessment questionnaires and numerous case examples can be used to prepare a performance profile that enables management to decide priorities, action improvements and monitor progress towards the achievement of performance levels and business results as good as, or better than, the best of the worldwide competition.

The book should be of particular interest to senior and middle managers, especially those managers having to cope with the management of change necessary to compete in an increasingly unstructured and competitive world market.

I am especially grateful to those many managers and supervisors who attended my leadership and coaching courses. Their experience and comments were invaluable in helping me to develop and refine my ideas on leadership style and decision-making. I would also like to thank those consultants, employers and civil servants who influenced my thinking during the development and field testing of a pilot version of the 'Investor in People Diagnostic Pack for use by Employers' and the 'Total Quality TEC Self Appraisal' for use by Training and Enterprise Councils.

I would like to express my appreciation to Mr Lyn Webb and Mr Phil Williams of the Gwent Training and Enterprise Council, the Monsanto Manufacturing plant at Newport, the Whitbread Beer Company at Magor and the Body Shop for permission to use case material. I am especially grateful to Mr Brian Smith of British Steel, and Mr Mark Canny, Mrs Angela Bush and Mr Paul Byard of Hills Industries for their assistance in the writing of case material. Special thanks are also due to Stuart Rees and Arwyn Reynolds for their contribution to the development of my ideas. I would also like to thank Mr John Pepper for sorting out some technical problems relating to the transfer of files from Deskmate to Microsoft Word.

Finally, I would like to dedicate this book to Dorothy, Nigel, Sheridan, Dan, Bethan, Melonie, Baden, Elaine and Thomas.

Bryan D Prescott

1

World class organizations

Customization, service and value for money equals customer satisfaction.

CUSTOMERS AND STAKEHOLDERS

In the face of a severe recession in the early 1980s many companies in the UK went out of business. Those that survived began looking closely at their businesses to identify where and how they could maintain and improve their performance and competitiveness. Initially this was driven by the need to reduce costs and improve productivity. There is, however, a limit to how far performance can be improved by cutting costs. To cut wages, for example, is one way of reducing costs but for most companies this is an unlikely option. Equally a competitor's cost advantage based on investment in technology and equipment is unlikely to be eroded without capital investment, which for many companies, especially small ones, may not be feasible.

During this period of analysis, some companies realized that improving productivity means not only raising the quantity of output per unit of input, it also means improving product design so that there is less rejection, thereby reducing the amount of stocks held to cover for rejects and the number of inspectors employed to check for defective work.

In the 1990s the environment has become more threatening for most organizations. Recession, automation, increasing competition and consumers who increasingly dictate the quality and specification of products pose major problems for traditional companies. There is a quantum shift taking place in our society, from a producer-led market to a consumer-led one. Consequently, companies most likely to survive the increasingly turbulent, competitive and uncertain times ahead are those that manage change effectively, listen to their customers and stakeholders, and invest in people and technology to increase productivity and flexibility.

In this book stakeholders are defined as investors, employees and the community. Whenever the word 'customer-centred' is used it should be interpreted as a management approach that aims to satisfy the needs and expectations of both customers and stakeholders. It aims to do this by using the practices and standards of the best of the competition at home and abroad as benchmarks against which to appraise and improve performance and business results.

A crucial aspect of the management of change is the leadership style and culture of the organization. Performance improvement initiatives driven from below by enthusiastic managers are doomed to eventual failure unless they are supported by senior management who lead by example. Fortunately, the message is slowly getting across that a customer-centred approach pays, and more and more managers are becoming convinced of its benefits. They realize that they can no longer make all the decisions themselves, and appreciate the need to tap the expertise of their people and release their creative talents. Managers are beginning to understand that it is no longer sufficient to regard the quality of the product on its own as the key to success. Most importantly, they realize that meeting the needs and expectations of customers and stakeholders – ie investors, the community and employees – is the best way to ensure continuous business success. In essence, this depends on an organization's ability to manage change, to customize its products and services quickly, and to provide value for money.

MEASURING THE RIGHT THINGS AT THE RIGHT TIME

The mission of WCOs is to satisfy the needs and expectations of their customers and stakeholders by ensuring that performance and business results are as good as, or better than, the best of the competition. They achieve this aim by appraising their performance and business results against the performance of the best of the competition at home and abroad (benchmarking) and using the results to improve their own performance.

WCOs realize that skilled and motivated employees are just as important to a company's success as are investors; they realize the importance of producing safe and environmentally friendly products that satisfy the needs of the community and the increasing number of ethical investors. They know that appraisal and continuous improvement of performance is the key to customer and stakeholder satisfaction.

To facilitate this continuous improvement process, performance measures that are customer-centred and integrated at business, companywide and operational levels are essential. Performance measures provide both management and employees with standards which focus their attention on what is most important to measure and on how well they are performing. The customer-centred measurement system (CCMS) shown in Figure 1.1, is designed to achieve this aim.

The CCMS also highlights the important distinction between external effectiveness (doing the right things) and internal efficiency (doing the right things in the right way – best practice). Another important, but often neglected, aspect of the measurement process is making measurements at the right time. Measurements at the end of a process, for example, are too late to prevent faults and errors that occur at an earlier stage. To be effective, measurements must be made on the process so that faults can be prevented or quickly rectified before they get to the customer.

At the business level, measures that relate to markets and finance are used to assess a company's performance and benchmarking is used to assess how well the company is doing in relation to competitors. Market measures at the business level include: absolute market share, relative market share, market share rank and share to largest competitor. Measures important to shareholders and other stakeholders in the company include: profitability, return on investment, earnings per share, price earnings, dividend yield, market value added and economic value added.

The four companywide performance measures are at the heart of the competitive battle. In the past ten years particular emphasis has been given to customer satisfaction and productivity. Greater emphasis

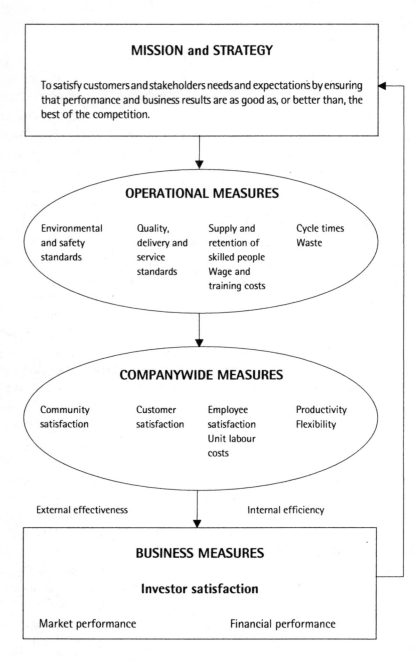

Figure 1.1 Customer-centred measurement system

is now being given to responsiveness to customers (flexibility) and impact on the community. Many companies are improving their flexibility by 'multi-skilling' their people and reducing cycle times. The ability to quickly customize environmentally friendly products and services is likely to be a decisive competitive factor in the years leading up to 2000.

Recently, there has been a significant change in competitive tactics as world class companies realize the importance of responding quickly to the public's demand for safer and more environmentally friendly products. Safety and pollution are now high on people's list of priorities as car exhaust fumes reach dangerously high levels in many of the world's major cities. In California, for example, tight controls on car exhaust emissions are forcing many car manufacturers to research and develop electric and hydrogen-powered cars. Clearly, companies that ignore their impact on the community do so at their peril.

Without an adequate supply of skilled people (qualified, competent and flexible) at all levels within the organization, no company can expect to remain in the top league for long. An important question, therefore, for all companies is: are we investing enough in our people's skills to meet operational requirements, change and contingencies? Qualified people usually have a mastery of core skills – mathematical skills, communication skills and information technology skills – which enable them to adapt quickly to a change of job or technology. Multi-skilling is another powerful means of improving people's flexibility and when combined with effective teamwork can lead to significant improvements in productivity and flexibility.

The growing importance of people to business success is convincingly argued by Karl Sveiby and Tom Lloyd in their book *Managing Knowhow* (1988). According to them, 'Europe's challenge of the 1990s is to learn how to export knowhow.' I agree with their conclusion. As living standards rise in Asia, South America and Africa, there is likely to be an increasing demand not just for manufactured goods but for all the services and skills which underpin a modern economy. Britain is particularly well placed to take advantage of these opportunities with its managerial, legal, design, training, military, public administration, communications, information technology and power generation knowhow.

For most companies the retention of key people, whose loss would have a significant impact on performance and who would be difficult to replace, is a key measure of how successful the company is at satisfying the needs and expectations of its employees. Dissatisfied employees are unlikely to plunge themselves with enthusiasm into a quest for excellence in all aspects of the business operation. A competent, adaptable and motivated workforce is, therefore, an essential part of the drive to achieve excellence in all aspects of the business. This is reflected in the increasing emphasis being given to investment in people and the development of cost-effective competence-based training.

A very important measure is, of course, unit labour costs – a combination of wage costs and productivity to give a statistic for total efficiency. Ideally this should be as good as, or better than, the best of the competition. In recent years, unit labour costs have improved in many industries in the UK because of improved productivity and, in many cases, relatively low wages.

What is crucially important, however, is that each measurement system is tailored to meet the particular needs of the organization and that it measures the right things at the right time. For this purpose, Figure 1.1 can be used by companies to develop their own customized integrated measurement system.

TEN PERFORMANCE MEASURES OF BUSINESS SUCCESS THAT CHARACTERIZE WORLD CLASS ORGANIZATIONS

The ten performance measures (PMs) are shown below. They are derived from the operational, companywide and business measures shown in Figure 1.1. These measures are themselves based on the standards and practices of many of the world's most successful companies.

The ten PMs enable companies large and small to appraise their performance against that of the best of their competitors and to use the results to prepare a performance profile – see Figure 12.1, page 142. The profile identifies strengths and weaknesses that can be used to decide priorities for further action.

A score of five indicates excellence in the application of the PM and that it is widely deployed within the organization. A score of zero means that either the measure does not apply or that you do not know the answer.

If you score less than five in a particular PM, a second level of appraisal should be conducted using the performance improvement criteria which include the critical inputs and processes underpinning each of the performance measures. The improvement criteria are contained in Chapters 2 to 11. The results of the second level of appraisal can be used by management to plan and implement the changes necessary to become a world class organization.

Ten Performance Measures that Characterize World Class Organizations

1. Senior management have made a commitment, which is circulated in writing throughout the organization, to create a world class organization.

    5 4 3 2 1 0

2. Strategy and business objectives are customer-centred, regularly reviewed and updated, and widely communicated within the organization.

    5 4 3 2 1 0

3. Management's leadership style encourages people to use their initiative and manage themselves and to accept personal responsibility for satisfying their customers.

    5 4 3 2 1 0

4. The supply of qualified, competent and flexible people is sufficient to meet operational demands, change and contingencies.

    5 4 3 2 1 0

5. Utilization of resources is as good as, or better than, the best of the competition.

    5 4 3 2 1 0

6. Productivity, unit costs and flexibility are as good as, or better than, the best of the competition.

    5 4 3 2 1 0

7. Customers rate the quality of products and services highly in relation to those of major competitors.

5 4 3 2 1 0

8. Employees express a high degree of satisfaction with the way they are managed, developed and their skills used.

5 4 3 2 1 0

9. The local community express satisfaction with the company's impact on environmental and safety matters and its involvement in community activities.

5 4 3 2 1 0

10. Investors express satisfaction with the company's business results which are as good as, or better than, the best of the competition.

5 4 3 2 1 0

Interpretation of scores:

40 to 50   Performance is on a par with the best of the competition.

30 to 39   Significant development need.

Less than 30   Major development need.

To avoid confusion with other definitions, a world class organization is defined in this book as:

An organization that is characterized by the ten performance measures and whose performance and business results are as good as or better than the best of the competition, that is, a score of 40 or more.

The emphasis given to each of the ten performance measures varies, of course, according to a number of variables. These include: senior management's leadership style and attitude, strategic objectives, the size and type of business and the culture within which the company operates.

World class organizations have enjoyed considerable success in recent years and for many of them the transition to a customer-centred strategy has led to new ways of operating their businesses. In the public sector, for example, market testing, compulsory competitive tendering, contracting work out and the Citizen's Charter are having a widespread impact. In the private sector organizations are much leaner with flatter management structures. Greater productivity and flexibility are being achieved by multi-skilling and the effective application of technology to reduce cycle times and waste and facilitate, for example, 'just in time' delivery systems. New ways of working are on the increase, for example, flexi-working, work-sharing, self-managed teams and home-based working.

As we approach 2000 the competitive battle will intensify and organizations that manage to survive will be those that are dynamic in managing change, listen to their customers, harness the talents of their people to continuously improve performance, and work closely with suppliers and key people in the community to tackle common problems. The faster a company can respond to change the more successful it is likely to be. Flexibility and speed of response are, therefore, critical strategic qualities which allow companies to cope with rapid external change. Conversely, traditional organizations that continue to do what they have always done, regardless of external change, will inevitably become less and less competitive since it is not possible to improve by doing the same things over and over again.

The chapters that follow provide more detail on each of the ten performance measures and contain appraisal criteria which may be used by companies to appraise and improve their performance, customer satisfaction and business results. It is for each company to decide how best to complete the appraisal criteria and how to use the results. The appraisal criteria are not set in concrete and companies may wish to use them as a framework from which to develop their own customized versions. In any case, the criteria should be reviewed from time to time and up-dated in line with evolving best practice and standards.

2

Customer-centred leadership

Performance measure '1'

Senior management have made a commitment, which is circulated in writing throughout the organization, to create a world class organization.

CHANGING LEADERSHIP STYLE

Increasingly managers are having to critically examine the way they manage people and involve them in the decision-making process. There are three particularly important reasons for doing this. First, managers are having to deal with a better educated and qualified workforce (workers are sometimes better qualified than the manager). Highly qualified and competent people do not take kindly to close supervision and control and are unlikely to accept autocratic decisions that affect them. Second, rapid technological change and unstructured work patterns mean that managers can no longer make effective decisions themselves. Third, there is growing evidence from the success of WCOs, especially in Japan, that empowering individuals and teams to manage themselves can produce remarkable improvements in performance. These pressures are forcing leaders to relinquish yet more control by delegating tasks and authority to individuals and teams.

It follows from the principle that people are most committed to decisions they make themselves that, whenever possible, leaders should delegate the making of decisions to individuals or teams. This could improve the quality of decisions and people's commitment to them. This is especially true when dealing with unstructured problems such as the commissioning of new plant, research work or the development of a new product. For example, a typical product development programme usually follows the following process:

Concept ⟶ **Development** ⟶ **Decision** ⟶ **Implementation**

Often each step in the process is carried out by specialist teams. In this type of system people tend to work in compartments with little or no opportunity to consult or exchange ideas. Experience has shown, however, that failure to consult widely before making decisions often causes delays in implementation and failure to achieve planned production targets. Conversely, the use of multi-discipline teams and wide-ranging consultation, including shop floor people, before critical decisions are made can increase commitment to decisions and achieve a better-than-planned-for performance.

According to the Employment in Britain survey (June 1993), one of the factors rated highly by people was the opportunity to show initiative and have some input in workplace decision-making, a finding that will come as no surprise to WCOs which operate voluntary team improvement activities. Despite the obvious fact that people at the coal-face know the processes best, know what the problems are and often have good ideas for solving them, many managers still fail to capitalize on the wealth of untapped talent at their disposal.

Paradoxically, in the 1990s, there has been a polarization of leadership styles. WCOs are characterized by leaders who focus on satisfying customer needs, encourage teamwork and involve employees in a process of continuous improvement of processes, products and services. Conversely, in some companies the drive for greater efficiency has led to an autocratic leadership style, which, when combined with 'downsizing' – reduction in manning and removal of layers of management – has caused an atmosphere of fear. Many employees fear losing their jobs, fear failing to achieve their targets and fear falling out with the boss.

'Management by fear' is characterized by leaders who impute the worst motives to subordinates, use threats, continuously increase targets, do not distinguish between explanations and excuses, never reward success, tell people they are lucky to be in a job and insist that they must do better. In such organizations competent people often lose their jobs to people who subscribe to management's values and leadership style.

Machiavelli's principles and techniques still flourish in many companies and there are still managers (I call them 'Mac' managers) who believe that the ends justify the means. They believe that they should never admit that they might be wrong, that morality and ethics are for the weak and that it is much better to be feared than liked. They make most, if not all, of the decisions and expect others to obey them without question. In stable conditions these tactics are often effective, at least in the short term. However, when faced with a rapidly evolving and unstructured situation where there are no 'experts', these tactics fail to deliver the products and services demanded by customers. The realities of competing in today's rapidly changing environment require flexible leadership, teamwork, empowerment and innovation. 'Mac' managers' days are numbered.

In February 1992 the Royal Society of Arts (RSA) published an interim report from its inquiry on 'Tomorrow's Company'. The inquiry was led by a team of executives from 25 leading businesses under Sir Anthony Cleaver, chairman of IBM UK. According to the RSA report, teamwork is vital to success. In this context, teamwork means investors collaborating with managers, managers collaborating with workers, companies collaborating with suppliers and all of them collaborating with the community outside. According to the report many British companies are deficient in most of them. The RSA recognizes that British industry is improving and its criticisms mainly concern the pace of change.

In the light of this report, it is worth recalling the words from a speech made in the late 1970s by the Japanese industrialist Konoke Matsushita to American businessmen: 'We are going to win and the industrialised West is going to lose out ... With your bosses doing the thinking while the workers wield the screwdrivers, you are convinced deep down that this is the right way to do business. For you the essence of management is getting the ideas out of the heads of the bosses and into the hands of labour ... For us the core of management is the art of mobilising and putting together the intellectual resources of all employees in the service of the firm.'

As pointed out in the RSA report, things are improving and many British-based companies are now amongst the world leaders for quality, teamwork and the involvement of people in the pursuit of excellence. Rank Xerox, for example, were the first winners of the European Quality Award (EQA) in 1992. Other examples of British-based companies which place customers at the centre of their strategy include: Rover, the Royal Mail, British Steel, Nissan and Honda.

CUSTOMER-CENTRED LEADERSHIP

A commitment to become a WCO represents a marked change for most organizations in leadership style and organizational culture, especially for traditional organizations which are characterized by:

- a failure to plan for the medium to long term
- a lack of vision and clear corporate beliefs
- control of people rather than empowerment and effective use of their talents
- making decisions based on opinions rather than facts
- allocating blame rather than looking for the causes of poor performance – many problems are caused at earlier points in a process than where they occur
- a failure to respond quickly to changing customer needs and expectations
- a failure to invest in plant and technology
- lack of effective communication and cooperation between departments and functions
- a failure to invest in people
- a failure to control processes and measure the right things at the right time.

This leadership style and culture was successful for many years but many companies are now finding to their cost that this is no longer the case because the conditions required for it to succeed are rapidly changing. For this leadership style and culture to succeed the following conditions are necessary:

- managers are able to make quality decisions themselves and employees are prepared to accept them
- there is little, if any, competition
- the market is producer-led rather than customer-led
- rates of technological change are slow
- world markets remain stable
- tasks and processes are structured and subject to very slow rates of change.

Unfortunately for traditional organizations, these conditions no longer prevail and the current worldwide situation is characterized by:

- competitors who empower and exploit the skills of their people in pursuit of excellence
- greater competition, especially from the Pacific rim
- relocation of companies to low wage economies to improve competitiveness
- the increasing demands of a customer-dominated market
- the growing power of ethical investors
- demands from the public for safe and environmentally friendly products
- the growing power of technology to increase productivity and flexibility
- re-engineering, which can lead to 'quantum leaps' in performance.

In recent years there has been a move towards a flexible and supportive leadership style which I call customer-centred leadership (CCL). At a senior level, CCLs respond flexibly to changing circumstances to create a leadership style, company ethos and strategy that enable managers to manage, train and empower their people to participate effectively in the process of achieving excellence in every aspect of the business.

CCLs promote teamwork and close cooperation with suppliers. They try to remove barriers and mistrust between different groups and sections and they involve themselves in the local community. If an organization is to be truly excellent in every activity, everyone must work together to ensure that customers' and stakeholders' needs and expectations are fully met. This requires a fundamental change to the traditional relationship between employees and the organization. For employees to be committed to the organization, the organization must be committed to its employees and senior management must lead by example.

All too often in the UK senior managers are awarded salary increases which are sufficiently contentious to make the headlines in many national newspapers, especially boardroom increases in recently privatized industries. It is hardly surprising, therefore, that many employees, who are expected to accept increases in line with inflation or productivity improvements, have no respect for senior management or loyalty to the organization. Such practices are hardly likely to create a motivated and highly productive workforce. They are more likely to reinforce the 'them and us' attitude that once afflicted most of British industry.

Unlike 'Mac' managers, CCLs lead by example; they develop and care for their people. They are seen to be fair and firm and to support their people in time of need. They consult with their people and seek ways of easing the trauma of redundancy by offering early retirement and voluntary redundancy as a first option. They provide guidance and counselling and help their people to re-train for other jobs. They realize that loyal and committed employees are just as important to business success as are investors. CCLs are not soft on productivity and flexibility – far from it. They realize that motivated and highly trained people who trust and have respect for their leaders are one of the keys to business success. Unfortunately, many companies either lack a consistent corporate code of ethics, or have a code which managers do not take seriously, especially in 'Mac' companies.

CHARACTERISTICS OF CUSTOMER-CENTRED LEADERSHIP

The characteristics of a customer-centred leader are shown below and can be used by senior managers to assess the extent to which their actions are creating a company ethos, strategy and management style that promote teamwork, innovation, empowerment and a process of continuous improvement that focuses on satisfying the needs and expectations of customers and stakeholders.

Performance Improvement Criteria
Customer-centred Leadership

For completion by senior managers

Appraisal criteria	Appraisal rating 5 = Strongly agree 1 = Strongly disagree

Do you:

- take steps to ensure that all employees know the company's mission and key objectives?   5 4 3 2 1

- support and show by your actions that you are committed to a customer-centred strategy?   5 4 3 2 1

- provide adequate resources and investment in people and technology to achieve world class standards?   5 4 3 2 1

- insist on people accepting personal responsibility for satisfying the needs of their customers?   5 4 3 2 1

- provide the tools, information, training and authority for people to participate in improvement and innovative activities?   5 4 3 2 1

- encourage recognition and reward for exceptional performance?   5 4 3 2 1

- ensure that there is a code of ethics which is enforced throughout the organization?   5 4 3 2 1

▓ support and actively participate in local
community activities? **5 4 3 2 1**

▓ encourage partnerships and close
cooperation with suppliers and the local **5 4 3 2 1**
community?

▓ keep people fully informed of the company's
operational performance and business results? **5 4 3 2 1**

Interpretation of results

40 to 50	Well on the way to becoming a customer-centred leader.
25 to 39	Significant development need.
Less than 25	Major development need.

3

Customer-centred strategy

Performance measure '2'

Strategy and business objectives are customer-centred, regularly reviewed, updated and widely communicated within the organization.

CUSTOMER-CENTRED STRATEGY

A customer-centred strategy aims to satisfy the needs and expectations of its customers and stakeholders by ensuring that performance and business results are as good as, or better than, the best of the competition. This is achieved by a process of measurement, appraisal and continuous improvement of all aspects of the business. Some aspects of a customer-centred strategy are:

Invest in people and technology	Accept cost as an investment and don't expect quick fixes. It is important to take a long-term view. The quest for excellence is a never-ending journey.
Develop clear beliefs and objectives.	Communicate beliefs and objectives to all employees. Try to instil a sense of purpose, commitment to business objectives and a pride in the organization.

Develop an appropriate management style and organizational culture.	Involve employees in decision-making. Managers should demonstrate their commitment to a customer-centred strategy by example.
Place the customer at the centre of the company's strategy.	Keep close to your customers and ensure that their needs and expectations are met.
Strive to achieve standards that are better than the best of the competition.	Benchmarking and audits. Customize and control processes – BS 5750/ISO 9000. Aim to do things right first time.
Involve every person in the organization in a process of continuous improvement.	Ensure that people are trained and have the tools, information and authority to participate effectively as individuals and in teams.
Measure the right things at the right time.	Customer-centred measurement system. Measurements on the process rather than at the end. Decisions based on fact rather than opinion.
Assess how effectively the organization is meeting the needs and expectations of its customers, shareholders, the community and its employees.	Market research, customer clinics, community surveys, shareholders' meetings, employee surveys.

Listening to customers and responding quickly to their changing needs, expectations and perceptions is a key characteristic of a WCO. Unfortunately, even once-successful companies sometimes become inward-looking, especially as they grow in size, and lose the close contact and feedback from customers that is necessary for success in an increasingly competitive market. For example, how many senior managers would be able to answer the following questions:

▨ Do you know why your customers buy from you and not from one of your competitors?
▨ Do you know what your customers think about the quality and reliability of your products and services in relation to your competitors?
▨ Do you know why other potential customers of yours buy from competitors rather than you?
▨ Do you know how your employees feel about the way they are managed, trained and their skills put to use?
▨ Do you know how the local community perceive the company in relation to safety, environmental issues and involvement in community activities?
▨ Do you know how the company is perceived on ethical matters by organizations that advise investors?

Organizations that know the answers to these questions have a competitive edge which they can use to promote their products and services. Increasingly, customers expect differentiated or personalized goods and services which means that companies have to be ever more responsive to their needs and expectations. As Mark Canny, managing director of Hills Industries, points out: 'it is not sufficient to just meet customers' needs and expectations, companies have to be pro-active and provide their customers with advice and guidance on design, specification and other product features'.

WCOs have good customer information systems. They are particularly good at measuring customers' and stakeholders' satisfaction with the company's performance and business results. They compare their own performance against the best of the competition and use the results to improve performance using a customer-centred measurement system such as that shown in Figure 1.1. This approach contrasts sharply with traditional measurement systems which are often complex, financially orientated and incoherent.

Despite all the complexity and jargon that surrounds it, marketing is simply finding out the needs of present and potential customers and then ensuring that those needs are met or exceeded. WCOs achieve this by focusing on four key areas of marketing – establishing customer needs, gathering information on customer trends, finding out what their competitors are doing and obtaining regular feedback from their customers. WCOs are likely to win the competitive battle for the following reasons:

- They keep close to their customers and take every opportunity to establish customers' needs, expectations and concerns.
- They take positive action to ensure that their customers' needs and expectations are fully met or exceeded.
- They exploit the power of the computer to amass information on customer trends and buying habits and produce customer profiles which enables them to offer customized services, exploit niche markets and respond quickly to changing fashions.
- They are particularly good at finding out what the competition are doing well and using the information to improve their own performance.
- They have a close empathy with customers and understand their likes and dislikes. They take steps to ensure that their information is relevant and up to date. As a result they know how to market and sell their products to their customers.

Because of their customer information system, WCOs are able to make informed decisions about whether they intend to compete on the basis of price or differentiation and whether they will target broadly across a number of market segments or focus narrowly on niche markets. At a time when customers and markets are ever more characterized by diversity and change, the faster a company can customize its products and services the more successful it is likely to be.

For example, according to a report in the *Sunday Times*, 29 January 1995, Ford claim that half the new car buyers by 2000 will probably be over 50 years old, and the number of drivers over 65 will have nearly doubled in 15 years. Accordingly, Ford decided to investigate the driving problems of old age. To help designers find out what it feels like for the over 65s, Ford designed the 'ageing suit' to constrict movement in the joints, hamper movement in the fingers and make touch less sensitive. Special glasses were also used to restrict vision.

The investigation is gathering information about the physical changes of ageing and the decline in eyesight. Older drivers take longer to focus, and often cannot focus at all on the instrument panel, they are more susceptible to glare, and take longer to recover from it. Reaction times are also slower and the over 65s find it difficult to divide attention between tasks. The investigation was followed by a survey of older drivers' attitudes and revealed that they were most worried about visibility and manoeuvring. This research is likely to affect the way Ford cars are marketed in the future. Apart from safety, which is already a major selling point, Ford are likely to place greater emphasis on simplicity.

Many firms are beginning to exploit the potential of the computer to provide information for effective decision-making. For example 'database marketing' (DM) is based on computer-generated shoppers' profiles that enable companies to target small groups of customers. The shoppers' profiles can be used, for example, to identify customers who never use the delicatessen. In America, mail shots offering customers special delicatessen discounts have resulted in 60 per cent of them taking advantage of the discounts. Follow-up studies have also shown that more than 30 per cent continue to use the delicatessen without the discounts. DM has many advantages over traditional marketing methods because it enables firms to target specific individuals or small groups at home. DM is likely to become a major marketing technique in the next ten years.

A critical factor in any business operation is customer loyalty. Recognizing this, some firms in America have launched what is called a 'passport programme' that identifies regular customers from its computer-generated shoppers' profiles and issues them with a 'passport' that entitles them to discounts on most products in the store. DM and the passport programme both depend on the effective use of computer technology to create customer profiles. DM is symptomatic of the explosive potential of computer databases to provide a customer information system that is increasingly being used in the battle to win new customers and retain customer loyalty.

Customers' expectations depend upon many factors but some of the major influences are:

- advertising
- promises from salespeople
- agreed specifications
- industry standards
- previous experience with a product or service
- experience with a competitor
- fashion shows
- concept cars on display at motor shows.

Marking time is insufficient because customers' expectations are becoming more demanding – they expect products to meet specification, to be delivered on time, to be reliable and they expect a first class after-sales service. As we move rapidly from a producer-dominated market to a consumer-dominated one, customization and customer service are becoming critical competitive tactics. Increasingly, companies which are customers of other companies (suppliers) are influencing the drive towards better quality and service by insisting that their suppliers achieve BS 5750/ISO 9000 or equivalent (for example Ford's Q1 quality system).

The trend towards customization of goods and services is likely to accelerate as technology makes it possible and customers become more knowledgeable and demanding. For example, the growth in satellite, cable and digital television is likely to usher in a huge expansion in pay-as-you-view programmes – an innovation that many customers, who resent having to pay for blanket services which do not meet their specific needs, are likely to welcome.

As companies strive to improve their efficiency in response to fierce competition, and customers demand value for money and better service, there is likely to be a huge increase in the next decade in home-based shopping, banking and cashless transactions. The popularity of tele-shopping, for example QVC on the Astra satellite, is a sign of things to come. As technology becomes more user-friendly and people overcome their computer phobia, the convenience of home-based shopping and banking will become irresistible, especially for people working long or unsocial hours, working mothers, the disabled, people without transport and elderly people.

Nowadays customers use a broad range of criteria to make a buying decision. These include, specification, after-sales service, reliability, maintenance costs, technical support and training. Successful companies meet these broader needs by adding value to the basic product or service and even traditional manufacturing companies are being forced by customers to become more service-orientated. Customization, value for money and service are critical competitive tactics.

For example, before entering the UK market, Daewoo conducted the biggest ever pre-launch survey by a car manufacturer to which almost 200,000 people replied. This information was used to ensure that customers' needs and expectations were met (customization) and resulted in the 'Daewoo Manifesto' covering, for example, value for money – electronic ABS, driver's airbag, side impact protection, power steering, engine immobilizer, security etching, mobile phone, delivery charges, full tank of fuel, 12 months' road tax and metallic paint all included in the quoted price. Similarly, the survey results were used to ensure that after-sales service met customers' needs and expectations – for example, free servicing for three years, three-year breakdown cover (AA), 30 day/1000 miles money back or exchange scheme, direct contact with mechanic who services the car, free courtesy car or pick-up and return of the car.

Realizing the importance of adding value and improving the quality and scope of customer services, many companies now offer:

- quicker and more reliable service and delivery
- longer opening hours
- products or services that nobody else offers
- on-site training
- distinctive image and personality
- on-site maintenance and repair
- technical support via the telephone
- courteous and professional customer service
- service standards for dealing with customers' complaints and cash refunds for failing to meet standards
- extended warranties and free insurance.

As the competitive battle intensifies, organizations that manage to survive will be those that are dynamic in managing change, listen to their customers, harness the talents of their people to continuously improve performance and work closely with suppliers and key players in the community on common interests. The following case example illustrates how a relatively small company has managed to do this:

Hills UK is a wholly owned subsidiary of Hills Industries Ltd, South Australia. A manufacturing plant opened in the UK in the early 1970s, and currently employs 110 people. The core business revolves around laundry products such as rotary dryers, ironing tables and clothes airers. The company also makes garden and industrial sprayers. Hills is a good example of a small company that is dedicated to meeting, and, if possible, exceeding the expectations of its stakeholders. Its 'policies' statement makes this clear:

- Business Planning

  We will meet the expectations of our stakeholders by building a respected position as the leading European laundry products supplier.

- Customer Relationships

  We will advance our relationships with our customers and raise their expectations.

- Supplier Relationships

  We will forge mutually beneficial partnerships with reliable suppliers.

- Employee Relationships

  We will, together, make Hills the best possible place to work.

- Monitoring Performance and Continual Improvement

  We will reduce waste by continually improving our systems and our reporting.

Mark Canny, managing director, is a firm believer in exceeding the expectations of his customers. He believes that conformance to specification is not enough and that it is necessary to be pro-active and advise customers on design and product features. For example, Hills advised one of its major customers to use a shade of green on one of the products it had ordered that matched the customer's corporate colour scheme. As a result of investment in plant and technology, which enables the colours of products to be quickly changed, customer response times have been reduced. This enables Hills to respond rapidly to customers' orders – an order received before lunch is sent out to the customer on the same day! Manufacturing flexibility is backed up by people flexibility. Mark Canny's vision is to achieve a position whereby all employees will be able to do every job on the process line. He realizes the practical difficulties involved, including people's resistance to change, but is well aware of the critical importance of a competent, motivated and flexible workforce in today's highly competitive market.

Paul Byard, manufacturing director, has responsibility for research and development and for orchestrating a process of continuous improvement. A notable feature of the quality improvement process is the various levels at which it takes place. Apart from the day-to-day improvements which occur through the normal management and control system, employees are encouraged to make suggestions for improvement to their section leader, who places their ideas on a 'board' on the factory floor for further action.

There is also a daily production meeting comprising representatives from various departments at which operational problems relating to, for example, materials, machines and training are discussed and corrective action agreed. A feature of the meetings is the rota membership system which ensures that cross-sectional issues are highlighted and discussed. Paul Byard delegates the chair to Dale Smart, section leader, who coordinates the activities of the meetings and liaises closely with Paul Byard. Multi-discipline project teams are formed to tackle difficult issues or problems that cannot be resolved by the production committee. These teams include operators, chargehands, section leaders, engineers, etc. Other problems, including customer complaints, returns and complaints made by phone, are dealt with by the product review committee.

The final step in this comprehensive approach to quality improvement is the research and development stage. Paul Byard devotes most of his time to gathering ideas for developing new products, reducing costs, cycle times and time-to-market of new products. Two important sources for generating ideas are a collaborative venture with the Cardiff Institute of Higher Education which is partly funded by Hills and a 'time-to-market programme' with the Welsh Development Agency aimed at reducing lead time to market. Sharing ideas and best practices with a network of 20 other companies (not in competition with Hills) is another valuable source of information. After selecting ideas for further development and evaluation, teams with a mix of relevant skills are formed to tackle specific projects.

This process can lead to what Paul Byard calls a 'mini-revolution'. In fact it is a good example of re-engineering in action. For example, some years ago the group management board authorized the replacement of existing plant and equipment with new plant and technology. This, together with other major changes in leadership style, the elimination of middle management and the introduction of flexible work practices, has resulted in market share increasing from 22 per cent to 36 per cent – establishing Hills as the UK market leader. Paul Byard firmly believes that the way forward is through continuous innovation, quality improvement and designing quality, safety and environmental standards into the product rather than inspecting faults out. Like Mark Canny, he too believes in exceeding customers' expectations by adding value to the product and keeping one step ahead of the competition.

Overall responsibility for training rests with Angela Bush, the personnel manager, who delegates responsibility for on-line training to section leaders who plan, organize and control training through the use of assessment sheets and control charts which show which job each person is competent to do and how much time each person has spent on particular jobs. These charts enable the section leader to decide when to move a person to another job for training and how many people are able to cover for particular jobs. As a minimum, the aim is to ensure that every employee on the shop floor is able to do the next job down the process line and the next job up. Standard operating procedures for each job are used for training purposes, and help to ensure that the well-known weaknesses of 'sitting by Nellie' are avoided. Employees share in the company's success through a profit-sharing scheme. A notable feature of the scheme is that everyone receives the same monetary benefit regardless of job position. People are kept fully informed on company matters – company policy documents and profitability figures, for example, are displayed in the works canteen.

Close relationships are maintained with suppliers to ensure an adequate supply of quality components and materials that are delivered on time. Although Hills is an accredited BS 5750/ISO 9000 organization, it does not demand the same of its suppliers. Mark Canny realizes that the cost of gaining and retaining BS 5750 accreditation is a significant factor for many small firms. To ensure that suppliers have adequate quality systems, Hills have trained six of their staff as quality auditors to conduct regular audits of suppliers' systems. This includes visits to observe the systems in action, the use of a questionnaire to gather relevant information and a short report on their findings. In the longer term, Hills are planning, in conjunction with their key suppliers, to implement a 'just in time' system.

Mark Canny serves on the board of the Mid-Glamorgan Training and Enterprise Council and is, therefore, actively involved in local training, education and enterprise initiatives. He also feels strongly about safety and environmental issues. Apart from regular internal safety audits, Hills finished runner-up in the Engineering Employers Federation National Safety Competition in 1994. Recently, an environmental policy was agreed and steps taken to progressively implement it.

The pay-offs that Mark Canny can point to so far from the company's efforts to satisfy the needs and expectations of its investors and customers by changing leadership style and reducing layers of management, investing in plant and people to improve productivity and flexibility, encouraging innovation and continuous improvement and developing close cooperation and exchange of information with suppliers and other companies are impressive. For example, in the last five years, turnover in the core business has doubled and Hills has moved from second place to become market leader in the UK with a 36 per cent share of the market.

Despite the worldwide success of WCOs, many companies have failed to exploit the benefits of a customer-centred strategy based on a total quality approach because of inappropriate management styles and attitudes. There is little point in exhorting employees to improve customer service, to do things right first time and to participate in quality improvement teams, if they are not given the tools, empowerment and support to do the job properly. Without effective management of people, customer-centred strategies are doomed to failure or, at best, partial success.

The characteristics of a customer-centred strategy are shown below and can be used by companies to assess how their strategy and corporate values compare with those of a WCO. A score of 5 means that you strongly agree with the statement and a score of 1 means that you strongly disagree.

Performance Improvement Criteria
Characteristics of a Customer-centred Strategy

For completion by senior management

Appraisal criteria	Appraisal rating 5 = Strongly agree 1 = Strongly disagree/don't know

▦ Our strategy is based on satisfying the needs
and expectations of investors, customers,
employees, suppliers, and the local   5 4 3 2 1
community.

▦ We have written policies covering:
- marketing   5 4 3 2 1
- customers' rights and complaints procedures   5 4 3 2 1
- safety and environmental issues   5 4 3 2 1
- relationships with the public and
  involvement in the community   5 4 3 2 1
- the rights, responsibilities, recognition
  and reward of employees.   5 4 3 2 1

▦ Our strategy is designed to achieve
excellence in all aspects of the business and
takes account of benchmarking as a means of
continuously improving performance.   5 4 3 2 1

▦ We have a means of effectively
communicating our mission, corporate
strategy and key business objectives to
all of our employees.   5 4 3 2 1

▦ We have established performance
measures that are customer-centred and
integrated at business, companywide and
operational levels – see Figure 1.1.   5 4 3 2 1

- We have developed advantages over our main competitors that attract customers; for example, brand name, efficient after-sales service.   **5 4 3 2 1**

- We regularly assess the sales and profit potential of different markets.   **5 4 3 2 1**

- We conduct regular market research of our customers' buying influences.   **5 4 3 2 1**

- We design the business to serve the needs of particular market segments.   **5 4 3 2 1**

- All customers are informed of the service standards they can expect from us – customers' charter.   **5 4 3 2 1**

- We assess, and act upon, customers' perceptions of the quality of our products and services in relation to that of our main competitors.   **5 4 3 2 1**

- We ensure that all employees are aware of feedback from customers.   **5 4 3 2 1**

- We have a means of obtaining relevant and up-to-date feedback from:
  - customers   **5 4 3 2 1**
  - investors   **5 4 3 2 1**
  - the community   **5 4 3 2 1**
  - employees   **5 4 3 2 1**
  - suppliers.   **5 4 3 2 1**

- We regularly review and up-date our policy and strategy.   **5 4 3 2 1**

Interpretation of results

90 to 110   Well on the way to achieving a customer-centred strategy.

70 to 89   Significant development need.

Less than 70   Major development need.

4

Management of people

Performance measure '3'

Management's leadership style encourages people to use their initiative and manage themselves, and to accept personal responsibility for satisfying their customers.

CUSTOMER-CENTRED MANAGEMENT

The emergence of WCOs with their emphasis on empowerment, teamwork, continuous improvement and partnerships is bringing about a change in the traditional role of managers and supervisors. Traditionally, managers make the decisions and tell their people what to do. In WCOs the management of people is focused on how best to manage and use people's skills and talents to continuously improve products, services and customer satisfaction.

Increasingly, managers have to orchestrate and coordinate a range of activities previously carried out by, for example, quality, training and personnel specialists. This calls for a much broader range of skills and knowledge than was previously the case. Managers are now expected to manage, motivate and train multi-skilled teams based on the concepts of customer service, empowerment and personal responsibility for quality. The role is a challenging one that requires management, coaching and enabling skills. Managers are expected to create the conditions in which multi-skilled teams can operate effectively by ensuring that they have the information, tools and training to do the task properly. I call this emerging role 'customer-centred management'.

Customer-centred managers (CCMs) have three inter-related roles in relation to the management of people. These are:

▓ managing people effectively
▓ enabling and supporting people to manage themselves
▓ training and developing people to promote competence and flexibility – see Chapter 5.

MANAGING INDIVIDUALS

CCMs realize that a manager's best guarantee of success is a motivated team committed to the achievement of goals. Conversely, lack of commitment to goals can lead to the creation of artificial problems as an excuse for not achieving them because subconsciously, if not consciously, people will want them to fail – the so-called self-fulfilling wish. CCMs strive, therefore, to gain commitment to key business objectives through wide-ranging consultation within the organization. They cascade corporate values right down to the lowest level and take positive action to ensure that the values are an integral part of the organization's operations and culture.

A mission statement to become a world leader in customer service is not very convincing if manning levels are cut and layers of management removed to such an extent that customer service suffers. Similarly, it is counter-productive to expect people and teams to perform tasks right first time without giving them the training, information and empowerment to act effectively. Paying lip service to world class standards can only lead to poor morale, lack of commitment to the organization and its goals, and poor customer service.

There is a considerable body of research which shows that people at work gain satisfaction from achievement, recognition, responsibility, advancement, challenging work, personal development and money. Research also shows that dissatisfaction at work is often caused by poor working conditions and poor leadership and supervision. Employees who have no trust or respect for their managers and supervisors are unlikely to join in an unending pursuit of excellence. Indeed, employee dissatisfaction is often a major cause of problems within organizations, for example:

- 'them and us' attitude
- high labour turnover
- a high level of customer complaints
- resistance to change
- lack of flexibility – it's not in my job description
- industrial disputes
- a high absenteeism rate.

In general, if people are told what has to be done and to what standard, they can plan, organize and carry out most of the work themselves with a minimum of supervision and control, providing they are given the information, tools, support and training needed to accomplish the task. Unfortunately, one of the problems with many managers is a tendency to supervise when it is not necessary. In my experience many people express dissatisfaction with the degree of control and supervision to which they are subjected. Too much supervision is counter-productive and causes frustration and resentment. It can also inhibit initiative and creativity.

Managers can do much to increase the motivation of their people by ensuring that their need for achievement, recognition, responsibility, development and fair play are met. Positive action that managers can take include:

- making sure that there are clear and measurable targets to be achieved
- ensuring that there is some personal responsibility for planning work and making decisions – delegation
- allocating tasks that are reasonably demanding and varied
- ensuring that people know when they are performing well and are given recognition for exceptional performance
- providing constructive criticism when people's performance is not up to standard
- involving people in decisions that affect them
- creating opportunities for self-development and progression

- ensuring that rules and regulations are applied consistently and fairly
- leading by example and showing concern for the welfare of their people.

CCMs insist on their people accepting personal responsibility for meeting the needs of their customers by ensuring that work passed on to the next person or customer is right first time. However, pressurizing people to improve their performance is doomed to failure unless management are prepared to provide them with the training and support they need to do their jobs properly.

The aim of CCMs is to reach a position where it can be said that the attitude of every worker is: I checked it, I got it right first time, the quality is fine, I satisfied my customer, I delivered on time, I'm proud of it. Unless employees accept personal responsibility for their work, programmes of continuous improvement will, at best, only be partially successful. One way of promoting personal responsibility for quality and creating a positive attitude towards the job is to use the job attitude profile (JAP – see Figure 4.1) that I developed when conducting research into core skills.

The JAP is designed to focus people's attention on critical tasks (doing the right things) and to enable them to assess and improve their attitude and performance. It can be used to assess attitudes in most non-supervisory jobs. It is especially effective if both the employee and his or her manager complete the profile and then compare and discuss the differences between the two appraisals.

MANAGING TEAMS

The complexity of most processes places them beyond the control of any one person. The best way to tackle complex or unstructured problems is to bring as much brainpower as possible to bear on them through the effective use of teams. The more people involved in a particular problem the more likely it is that a quality solution will emerge. For example, consider a manager who has to decide on the pattern of distribution from three factories – A, B and C – to meet the demands of three warehouses

Non-supervisory jobs

Appraisal criteria	Appraisal rating		
I prepare, organize and check tools, materials and equipment before starting a job.	Always **5**	Mostly **3**	Seldom **1**
I correct errors as they occur and do my best to get things done right first time.	Always **5**	Mostly **3**	Seldom **1**
I finish my work to standard and on time.	Always **5**	Mostly **3**	Seldom **1**
I check that my work is up to standard before passing it on to the next person/customer.	Always **5**	Mostly **3**	Seldom **1**
On completing my work, I leave my workplace in a safe and tidy condition.	Always **5**	Mostly **3**	Seldom **1**
I help and support my colleagues when they need it.	Always **5**	Mostly **3**	Seldom **1**
When people deliver work to me which is below standard, I tell them about it as soon as possible	Always **5**	Mostly **3**	Seldom **1**
If I think of a way of improving performance, I let my boss know about it.	Always **5**	Mostly **3**	Seldom **1**

Interpretation of results

35 to 40	Positive job attitude.
20 to 34	Significant training need.
Less than 20	Major training need.

Figure 4.1 Job attitude profile

– X, Y and Z. The total demand from the three warehouses is equal to the total capacity of the three factories:

Factory	Capacity (units per month)	Warehouse	Demand (units per month)
A	3000	X	6000
B	5000	Y	3000
C	6000	Z	5000
	14,000		14,000

The transport costs for delivering from each factory to each warehouse are as follows:

		Warehouses		
		X	Y	Z
	A	3	7	4<<< Transport costs in £ per unit
Factories	B	6	10	9
	C	4	9	6

The manager's task is to distribute units from the factories to meet the warehouse demands at minimum transport cost. Are costs likely to vary significantly depending on the pattern of distribution? This problem is best tackled as follows:

This pattern of distribution to the warehouses gives a total transport cost of:

3000 × 3	=	£9000 (units × cost per unit)
3000 × 6	=	£18,000
3000 × 9	=	£27,000
2000 × 9	=	£18,000
3000 × 6	=	£18,000
Total transport costs	=	£90,000

This represents the maximum transport cost. Before looking at the minimum cost solution, see if you can work it out for yourself. This example illustrates that transport costs can vary significantly depending on the pattern of distribution and is a good example of the fact that teams are more effective than individuals when tackling unstructured problems. I have found on leadership courses that the more people there are on the course the more likely it is that one of them will work out the minimum cost solution. In practice there is always a spread of solutions from maximum to minimum.

The minimum transport cost solution

	Demand 6000 X	Demand 3000 Y	Demand 5000 Z	Cost in £ per unit
Capacities A 3000	3	7	4 (3000)	
B 5000	6 (2000)	10 (3000)	9	
C 6000	4 (4000)	9	6 (2000)	

3000 × 4	=	£12,000
2000 × 6	=	£12,000
3000 × 10	=	£30,000
4000 × 4	=	£16,000
2000 × 6	=	£12,000
Total transport cost	=	£82,000

The use of the team approach to problem solving has many advantages. For example:

- A greater variety of problems may be tackled which are beyond the capability of any one individual.
- Teams are more likely to generate high quality decisions than people working alone, especially when tackling unstructured problems.
- Problems are exposed to a greater diversity of knowledge, skill and experience.
- Effective teamwork helps to boost motivation and morale.
- Problems which cross departmental or functional boundaries can be dealt with more easily.
- Team recommendations are more likely to be implemented than individual contributions.

WCOs exploit these advantages by empowering teams to tackle a wide range of tasks and problems. If teams have a clear understanding of what they are expected to do and to what standard, they can plan, organize and do most of the work themselves with a minimum of supervision, especially when combined with multi-skilling. The extreme example of this process is the formation of self-managed teams (SMTs).

Effective teamwork throughout an organization is essential. Much of the culture in the West has been one of independence with little sharing of ideas and information. Fortunately this is changing and the emphasis is now on meeting customers' needs through teamwork, cooperation and partnership. Where there is an atmosphere of support and trust, information is shared rather than hidden. Cooperation amongst the team is likely to create higher morale as individuals contribute from their own pool of experience. Managers should encourage this process of sharing information and of helping each other to overcome particular problems or difficulties. A supportive team committed to common goals can lead to significant improvements in performance.

An organization is not likely to achieve peak performance from a collection of teams which are not cooperating and coordinating effectively. One way of overcoming this problem is by clearly defining the customer/supplier relationships within the organization so that teams know exactly what their customer's needs are and get fast feedback when they are not meeting them. Regular meetings between team leaders to discuss issues relating to coordination and cooperation amongst teams is essential.

Effective communication within teams, between teams and the organization as a whole, is crucial if excellence in all aspects of the business is to be achieved. People are most concerned about the future because it holds the key to their future security and prosperity. They want to hear about the company's plans for the next few years; they want to know how those plans are likely to affect them. Employees are interested in how profitable the company is but they see things differently from management who view profits as a measure of how well they are running the business. Employees, on the other hand, see profits as an indicator of future pay levels. All too frequently leaders give an inspirational message about organizational changes and board appointments, but they use charts and statistics showing profits, sales, costs and output which are often presented in a language employees do not understand.

Some of the options open to leaders who want to communicate more effectively with their people include:

- regular departmental meetings between managers and team leaders
- managers adopting an open communications style
- more consultation before decisions are made by senior managers that affect teams and individuals
- more information about the company's plans and business performance presented in a form that makes sense to people on the shop floor

▓ surveys to establish how employees feel about the way they are managed and their skills put to use. The results can be used to identify and discuss common issues that people feel strongly about (see Chapter 9).

ENABLING AND SUPPORTING PEOPLE TO MANAGE THEMSELVES

CCMs possess the ability to select a leadership style best suited to particular circumstances. They know when to be autocratic and when to delegate. They are particularly good at creating the conditions that enable people to use their creative talents in pursuit of excellence through a process of continuous improvement and innovation.

Faced with change and an increasingly unstructured situation, managers often find it difficult to relinquish control of the decision-making process which they sometimes regard as an abdication of management's responsibility. This can be an acute problem for middle managers and supervisors in WCOs, where the role of the manager and supervisor is more akin to that of a coach and enabler.

The ability to decide which leadership style to use is a key management skill and I have observed over the years that many leaders tend to adopt a particular leadership style and apply it with little variation to all situations. Conversely, other managers use a range of styles – sometimes they are autocratic, sometimes they consult and sometimes they delegate. This raises interesting questions. For example:

▓ What leadership styles are there?
▓ Does it matter which leadership style is used?
▓ Are some styles more effective than others, and if so why?

In my book *Effective Decision-Making,* I identified five major leadership styles. These are:

The autocratic leadership style – A

In this case, the leader makes most decisions based on his knowledge and understanding of the task or problem. The leader does not consult with others or seek additional information from other sources. The assumption is that the leader has sufficient information and skill to generate high quality decisions.

In structured stable situations where the same thing is done over and over again successfully, there is little point in delegating to other people since the manager is quite capable of making quality decisions alone. To consult or delegate would only increase the time and cost of making decisions and unless there is a good reason to justify the use of delegation, for example to improve motivation, morale or commitment, the autocratic style is more appropriate. There is little point in empowering people to make decisions when there is no clear reason for doing so. Similarly, there is no point in delegating the decision-making process to individuals or teams unless they are competent to make quality decisions and are motivated to do so.

The information seeking autocratic leadership style – I

In this case, the leader does not possess sufficient information to generate a high quality decision but knows what information is required and where to get it from. Before asking for the information required, the leader may or may not tell others why he needs it. In most cases, the leader simply asks for the information required before making the decision himself. Unfortunately, leaders often assume that they are competent to make decisions alone when in, fact, they are not.

The 'A' and 'I' styles are still widely used, especially in traditional firms which have not yet been convinced of the benefits of delegation, teamwork and empowerment. The important point to understand is that CCMs use whatever style is appropriate for dealing with the particular situation. When tasks are highly structured and decisions have to be made quickly, the autocratic styles are the right ones to use on quality, time and cost grounds. Conversely, when tasks are unstructured and problems complex, it is much more effective to consult or delegate to teams and hence gain the benefit of other people's expertise.

Consultative leadership style – C

The 'C' style is characterized by leaders who tap the expertise of other people but who retain control over the final decision themselves. The leader explains the task or problem to others and gives them the information they need to generate and evaluate options. The leader may act as chairman or discussion leader or leave the group to work on their own. The leader evaluates the information gathered from the consultative process, including recommendations which may or may not be accepted by the leader. Sometimes the leader may commission people to conduct an investigation and report back. The leader then discusses the report's findings before making the final decision himself.

Clearly, if there is a clash of interest between the leader and others, the leader must retain control of the decision-making process. This means that the 'D' leadership style is ruled out. The 'C' leadership style is widely used in 'knowledge-based organizations' such as the civil service, local government and consultancy firms. With increasing rates of change, leaders are less likely to be capable of making quality decisions themselves and the more brain power that can be brought to bear on the problem, the greater is the chance of a quality decision being generated.

The negotiation leadership style – N

The aim of this leadership style is to reconcile differences and for the parties involved to agree a mutually acceptable solution. The leader normally provides sufficient information for the negotiations to proceed in a sensible manner. Before entering into negotiations, the leader may consult widely with others in the organization in order to generate and evaluate a range of options and decide what is and what is not acceptable to the company. The 'N' style is used when the other party is not likely to accept the leader's decision based on consultation. It is most frequently used when dealing with industrial relations problems or when negotiating contracts with staff, suppliers, sub-contractors and consultants.

The delegation leadership style – D

In this case, the leader empowers individuals or groups to make decisions on a range of work-related tasks such as planning, problem solving and continuous improvement. To perform this difficult task, it is essential for management to provide the team or individual with the tools, information, authority and training to do the task well. Support and guidance from management is, therefore, essential. Examples of this type of delegation include, semi-autonomous work groups, self-managed teams and home-based workers.

Clearly, if there is a clash of interest between the manager and employees, the 'D' style is ruled out. Fortunately, there are many aspects of running a business where there is a common interest between management and employees. People on the shop floor often have a better grasp than managers do of the causes of poor performance and how best to eliminate them. Unfortunately, in traditional organizations, employees are still excluded from the decision-making process, thereby failing to exploit their experience and creative talents. The good news is that more and more organizations are adopting a customer-centred strategy based on teamwork and empowerment because they realize that involving employees in planning and problem solving can lead to significant improvements in performance and motivation.

One important conclusion arising from the principle that people are most committed to decisions they make themselves is that, whenever possible, managers should delegate the decision-making process. Unfortunately, many leaders fail to realize that their responsibility is to use people effectively rather than to retain control through close supervision and retention of the decision-making process. If performance can be improved by relinquishing some control over people, then so be it. Other leaders who recognize the relationship between performance and empowerment are often prevented from capitalizing on this because of organizational constraints.

Delegation often fails to deliver the expected benefits because employees are either not properly trained for the task or they do not receive the information, empowerment and support from management needed to operate effectively. There is little point in delegating to teams or individuals if they are not competent to do the job. Fortunately, most employees, given the right training and support, are capable of self-management on a wide range of work-related tasks.

The guidelines below can be used by managers to help them develop the skill of deciding which leadership style to use in particular circumstances.

CCMs use the full range of leadership styles but, whenever possible, they delegate tasks to teams or individuals. They do this to improve the quality of decisions, especially when dealing with unstructured tasks and problems, to motivate people and to release their creative talents. A key distinguishing mark, therefore, of CCMs is their ability to adjust their leadership style according to the abilities and commitment of their people and the demands of the task. The aim is to make quality decisions and improve performance and not to retain control. This skill is particularly important at a time of rapid change in customers' expectations, the introduction of new technology and the emergence of a more highly qualified and competent workforce that does not respond well to tight control and close supervision.

Selecting a leadership style most likely to generate effective decisions

Leadership style	Factors to take into account
A and I	Leader is competent to make a quality decision alone or has access to the information needed to do so.
	The task is highly structured and can be solved by the leader alone.
	Others are not competent to make a quality decision. This rules out C and D.
	People are prepared to accept leader's decision. This makes A or I possible.
	Decisions have to be made quickly. This normally rules out C and D.
C	The leader is not able to make quality decisions alone. This rules out the use of A and I.

Others are not likely to accept decisions that affect them without consultation. This also rules out A and I.

There is a conflict of interest between leader and others – this rules out the use of D.

Others are competent to make decisions – this makes C or D possible.

Morale and team spirit are low – participation would help to gain greater commitment to decisions and improve motivation.

N	Others will not accept leader's decision on the basis of consultation. This rules out A, I and C.
	There is a clash of interest between the leader and others. This rules out the use of D.
D	Leader is not competent to make quality decisions alone
	The task is unstructured – the more brainpower that can be brought to bear on the problem, the more likely it is that a quality decision will be generated.
	Others are competent to make decisions – this makes the use of D possible.
	There is no conflict of interest between the leader and others – the leader can, therefore, delegate the task to others.
	Time and cost are not critical. This makes the use of delegation acceptable.

> The organization is committed to a strategy
> of empowerment of people to solve
> problems and make decisions themselves.

The following case example illustrates the benefits that can be gained from effective communications, teamworking, empowering people to solve problems and investing in people's skills:

The Monsanto plant at Newport in Gwent is part of the worldwide Monsanto Chemical Company. The Newport plant produces speciality chemicals for more than 1000 customers worldwide. Output from the Newport plant ends up in products ranging from tyres to detergents, and paints to medical goods.

Monsanto have been established in Newport for more than 40 years, but particularly during the 1980s international competition increased considerably and management clearly saw the need to meet sharply higher production, quality, environmental, safety and productivity targets. Absolutely central to meeting the demanding new targets was Monsanto's commitment to investing in their people through a long-term programme to build the skills of all employees. Structures and communications were set up so that all skills would be effectively used. Action taken included:

- single status working for everybody on site
- multi-skilling and flexible working
- empowering individuals to solve problems on-the-spot
- personal training plans for everybody on site
- breaking down 'them and us' barriers, building good communications and teamworking
- practical training programmes to develop and keep up to date key technical skills, and also build the relevant personal and business skills to meet increasingly demanding customer requirements in the future.

Monsanto's policy is to build for the longer term – both in its plant and in its people. The company needs to keep its quality, safety and productivity standards up to consistently high levels, yet retain the flexibility to meet market demands quickly.

Monsanto was involved in the pilot phase of Investors in People within Gwent. The national standard had much common ground with what Monsanto saw as straightforward good management. The pay-offs Monsanto can point to so far from its efforts to train staff well and make good use of their skills include:

- productivity rising by 67 per cent over the past five years
- very low labour turnover and absenteeism
- meeting tough production, quality and environmental targets with fewer staff.

In the UK, many companies use consultative meetings to discuss with employees a whole range of welfare issues and some are now beginning to broaden the agenda to include business matters. Unlike the requirements of the Social Chapter, the meetings tend to be informal, with management setting the agenda. The advantages of this type of arrangement are that, unlike works councils, they are low cost, avoid bureaucratic machinery and can be called at short notice to discuss important welfare and business matters. In this way, employees and management are able to discuss serious business issues together and, at the same time, employees gain a sense of satisfaction from their involvement in the making of decisions.

Technology has made it possible for more people to work at home and, to a large extent, manage themselves. I was a home-based worker myself and I can vouch for the cost savings and increased productivity that can result from this mode of working. But, to be effective, people need to be carefully selected because some people do not respond well to working from home for a variety of reasons – for example, the isolation and lack of support, which people at work do not normally experience, can be a problem.

Home-based working is a pattern of work which will undoubtedly be more important in the future, particularly as information technology frees work from fixed sites and the traditional office environment. It is an arrangement which will be attractive and helpful to people whose family commitments make it difficult for them to go to the office every day and for people with disabilities and health problems. In these situations, managers need to provide appropriate support facilities, otherwise people become isolated and out of touch to such an extent that they lose their motivation and sense of belonging to the organization. Electronic mail, newsletters, helplines and occasional group meetings at a central location to discuss relevant issues may help to overcome these problems.

Many managers are finding it difficult to adjust to the enabling and support role, especially since many companies are themselves struggling to define what the role should embrace. What is clear, however, is that the emerging CCM role is more akin to that of a coach and enabler than the traditional autocratic management role. It is more about creating the conditions in which people can use their skills in pursuit of excellence. This means investing in people and providing them with the information, tools and training to do the task properly.

CCMs' support role is becoming increasingly important as they are having to become more involved in helping customers and suppliers solve their problems by providing better service, technical assistance and on-site training. More and more companies are beginning to realize that success in winning and retaining business is as much about solving customers' problems as providing traditional products and services. Without doubt the support/consultancy role of CCMs is bound to increase as customers demand ever better services and technical assistance. Similarly, closer cooperation and partnership arrangements with suppliers is also placing additional demands on managers to provide appropriate support facilities.

The chart below can be used by managers and team leaders to assess how their performance measures up to that of a customer-centred manager.

Performance Improvement Criteria
Management of People

For completion by middle managers and team leaders

Appraisal criteria	Appraisal rating 5 = Strongly agree 1 = Strongly disagree

Do you:

have a clear understanding of the
organization's mission and key objectives?   5 4 3 2 1

communicate the organization's mission
and key objectives to all of your people?   5 4 3 2 1

involve your people in planning and
problem solving?   5 4 3 2 1

ensure that people know what they have
to do and to what standard in order to
satisfy their customers?   5 4 3 2 1

allocate tasks to people that are
reasonably demanding and challenging?   5 4 3 2 1

ensure that people are told when
they are performing well and given
recognition for exceptional
performance?   5 4 3 2 1

give constructive criticism when people's
performance is not up to standard?   5 4 3 2 1

insist on people accepting personal
responsibility for satisfying their customers?   5 4 3 2 1

░ keep supervision and control to a
minimum?   **5 4 3 2 1**

░ apply rules and regulations firmly and
fairly to all?   **5 4 3 2 1**

░ encourage open communication and
accessibility?   **5 4 3 2 1**

░ lead by example?   **5 4 3 2 1**

░ employ a range of leadership styles in
response to particular circumstances?   **5 4 3 2 1**

░ delegate tasks and authority to teams
and individuals when appropriate?   **5 4 3 2 1**

░ provide teams with the tools,
information, training and authority
they need to manage themselves
effectively?   **5 4 3 2 1**

░ encourage employees to use their
initiative and to participate in a
process of continuous improvement?   **5 4 3 2 1**

Interpretation of results

65 to 80   Well on the way to becoming a customer-centred
                   manager.

50 to 64   Significant development need.

Less than 50   Major development need.

5

Training and developing people

Performance measure '4'

The supply of qualified, competent and flexible people is sufficient to meet operational demands, change and contingencies.

INVESTMENT IN PEOPLE

Business success lies in the drive for enhanced performance through improving quality, productivity and flexibility. Though these can be improved through the effective use of materials, equipment or technology, ultimately it is the effective development and use of people's skills that is most important. For example, a series of detailed studies comparing similar businesses in Germany and the UK revealed the following:

- German plants had fewer breakdowns and far less downtime.
- Much of the difference in machine and product reliability came from the German operators' ability to recognize quality problems themselves.
- German furniture factory operatives were more broadly skilled, cleaning their own machines and able to take part in preventative maintenance.
- German workers had a broader range of skills and responsibilities.

Unfortunately, in my experience, many managers pay lip service to training while allowing unsystematic and inefficient training practices to flourish. It is hardly surprising, therefore, that the UK lags behind their main competitors in the training and development of people at work. The situation in the UK has declined sharply since 1981 when most of the Industry Training Boards, which were empowered to raise a levy on employers to promote good training practice, were abolished by the government. However, recent developments such as the creation of Training and Enterprise Councils, the development of national vocational qualifications (NVQs) and the introduction of the Investors in People award should improve the quality and quantity of training provision in the UK. The following case example illustrates the benefits of investing in people and empowering them to solve problems and improve performance themselves:

The Whitbread Beer Company's Magor Brewery is one of the company's two major UK brewing plants. It has the capacity for brewing and packing 1.8 million barrels of ales and lagers, which include such well-known names as Heineken Lager, Stella Artois, Whitbread Best Bitter, Welsh Bitter and Murphy's Irish Stout.

Employing around 380 staff, the brewery has ambitious targets for achieving continuous improvement to quality and productivity performance. These targets are being met through integrated programmes to invest in modern equipment, enhance working practices, and develop the skills of everybody on site. Central to these programmes are:

- empowering staff to solve problems, make decisions and continually improve performance themselves
- fostering excellent teamwork
- reducing layers of management
- promoting greater operating flexibility.

The company has worked closely with the Gwent Training and Enterprise Council (TEC) since the TEC was formed. An example of this partnership has been TEC support for a successful and innovative Open Learning Centre. This centre offers wide-ranging and highly cost-effective training, particularly for shift workers.

Discussions with the TEC led on to the Investors in People award. The company was interested not so much in changing well-established policies, but in using the national standard as a benchmark. This allowed an objective review of progress so far, encouraged one or two plans to be brought forward, and gave inputs to further planning. So, after a six-month joint programme with Gwent TEC the Magor Brewery was recognized as an Investor in People in October 1992.

The Whitbread commitment is to continuing, long-term development for the Magor Brewery: investing in people is one part – a key part – in carefully integrated plans. Benefits so far from this philosophy include:

- productivity gains of 25 per cent
- a 'leaner, flatter' managerial structure
- meeting ambitious quality targets
- recognition throughout the group for its leading role in 'people development' and business performance.

The days have long gone when a person entered a firm at 15 and progressed steadily along a career path with the same firm until retirement. Nowadays, it is not enough to do the current job well; flexibility and multi-skilling are essential if products and services are to evolve quickly enough to meet the ever-increasing demands and expectations of customers and investors. A firm's most valuable asset are the skills of its people. But these skills do not come cheaply and it is no longer possible to make do with the ad hoc unsystematic training practices which still prevail in many organizations.

Companies which are in the process of improving their responsiveness to customers have already discovered that, whilst it is in part about developing flexible systems and re-organizing operations, what really matters is people. If employees are not developed in a way that achieves a customer focus, little improvement will be seen because, in the final analysis, it is people and their attitudes to customers which make the systems and procedures work. Consequently, the way that a company manages, develops and uses its people's skills is a critical factor in achieving greater flexibility, improved productivity and customer satisfaction. The training and development role of CCMs is, therefore, becoming increasingly important in the fight to develop a competent and flexible workforce that is able to match the best of the competition and ultimately challenge the world's best.

Sveiby and Lloyd in their book *Managing Knowhow* claim that people in the Western world will soon be spending more on solutions to problems than on physical products and that most of the recent growth in US employment has come from this sector. They also point out that more and more companies, large and small, are evolving into knowhow companies which are critically dependent on the skills and knowledge of their employees. Investment in people is, therefore, vital to the current and future success of these companies, as it is to any organization wanting to satisfy its customers by producing value for money products and services. Examples of knowhow companies include: law firms, accountancy firms, computer service companies, advertising agencies, brokers, universities, R&D, hospitals, theatres, government departments, newspapers, high-tech companies and consultancy organizations.

According to Tom Peters in *Thriving on Chaos*,

> The older industrial economies have two options: They can try to match the wages for which workers elsewhere are willing to labour. Or they can compete on the basis of how quickly and well they can transform ideas into incrementally better products. Today's and tomorrow's winning hand is becoming increasingly clear: quality and flexibility. Essential to them both are smaller units and highly skilled workers serving as the chief source of continuous improvement in goods and services.

RECRUITING THE RIGHT PERSON FOR THE RIGHT JOB

The recruitment planning process involves predicting, in the short to medium term a firm's staff requirements, and ensuring that the recruitment process is cost effective and recruits the right people at the right time.

Recruitment planning only makes a contribution to the business if it aids management in meeting the demands of their jobs. The emphasis should, therefore, be on critical recruitment areas, for example, people who are not easy to replace and skills that are critical to the organization's business success. In many organizations people are the most important asset of all, and this is especially true in 'knowledge-based companies' which can ill afford the loss of a key worker whose knowhow is vital to the success of the firm. Questions that should be addressed include:

- Are there any areas or key groups where staff shortages are most likely to affect the company's plans?
- Are there any jobs/skills where recruitment is particularly difficult?
- Which jobs/skills have a long training period?
- In which areas have labour costs been rising most steeply?
- Which jobs/functions directly affect profitability?
- Which job categories have a high rate of staff turnover?
- Which job categories have a high rate of absenteeism?
- Which employees have an in-depth knowledge of the company which it would be difficult to replace?
- Which jobs of importance have no trained successor available?
- How important are academic qualifications to the business?

Loss and recruitment of staff is an expensive business. Yet, if my experience is anything to go by, many companies' recruitment policies and practices leave much to be desired. Managers, who have not been trained in recruitment or testing techniques, are often given responsibility for interviewing prospective candidates. Tests are frequently administered by unqualified people who fail to follow test procedures which are essential for reliability. And, worst of all, enthusiastic amateurs devise their own tests with no regard for validity.

Loss of staff is a vital factor in all businesses. Though there are common and transferable skills, each person takes with him when he leaves, a knowledge of the company and the job, which can rarely be purchased outside the firm. Fully effective operation is thus reduced, and continues for a period at a reduced level, even when a suitable replacement is found. A positive outcome, therefore, for a WCO is employee satisfaction. Well-qualified and competent people are essential to compete on the world stage, and one way of keeping them is by trying to satisfy their needs and expectations, as far as is reasonably practical. It is also important to remember that, apart from wage costs, one of the most important factors in attracting inward investment is the skills of the local labour force.

CUSTOMIZED COMPETENCE-BASED TRAINING

Traditionally, training has been perceived as taking place away from the workplace in training centres or at college. Evidence of achievement has been reflected in qualifications gained through a course of study and end assessment which was mainly theoretical and sometimes unrelated to competence at work.

During the period 1970 to 1982, some of the Industry Training Boards (ITBs) were increasingly concerned about the efficiency and effectiveness of current training provision. All too often training providers and colleges responded to varying training needs with standardized training packages and fixed start and finish times. Many industries were also experiencing growing competition from abroad and greater demands from their customers for better quality products and services. New technology was also having a major impact on work patterns and skill requirements.

As a result of these concerns, some of the ITBs investigated the efficiency and effectiveness of current training methods, particularly the relevance of off-the-job training to competence at work and the effectiveness of 'sitting by Nellie' training, that is, placing a person for training under the guidance of an experienced worker. The main findings were:

- 'Nellie' training, although it can sometimes be very effective, has many failings.
- Off-the-job training is very expensive and often not relevant to competence at work – for example, craft apprentices spent hours mastering the use of a file which was no longer used at work.
- There was too much emphasis on theory, end assessment and time serving.
- There was no opportunity for adults to gain formal recognition of the skills, knowledge and experience they had acquired at work.
- The training system was failing to produce the competent and flexible people demanded by rapid change, greater competition at

home and abroad, new technology and customers' growing demands for better quality products and services.

Two major conclusions were: first, there was a need for greater responsiveness to trainees' needs (customized training); and second, training and assessment should take place at work on the actual tasks themselves (competence-based training), unless it was not practical to do this, for example if:

- there is a high risk of an accident
- an error by a trainee could cause expensive damage to plant or equipment
- the task involves sensitive customer contact skills
- the task occurs at irregular times (faults) and cannot be scheduled or simulated on the job
- there is a considerable amount of knowledge and principles to be mastered.

In these cases, off-the-job training and testing is often the only way to impart the skills, knowledge and understanding required for competent performance at work.

By 1981 there was sufficient evidence to show that customized training based on competence at work had many advantages over the traditional approach. For example:

- The training was more relevant since it was based on an identification of training needs at organizational, team and individual levels.
- There was a reduction in the cost of training – most training took place at work and there was no 'fixed' training times. Training ended when the trainee was assessed as being competent.
- A more consistent performance was achieved because trainees were assessed on their ability to do the actual task or job to operational standards.
- Motivation was improved because trainees could see the relevance of their training.
- There were measurable improvements in operational performance – fewer delays, fewer defects, less waste and fewer customer complaints.

Since then, further research and development work, particularly on competence-based qualifications known as National Vocational Qualifications (NVQs), has confirmed the benefits of competence-based training. For example:

- it provides an immediate pay-off – improved performance and ability to work with decreasing degrees of supervision
- it reduces the need to release key people from their jobs for protracted periods
- it enables trainees to benefit from the expertise of on-the-job coaches/instructors who know the tasks and jobs far better than off-the-job trainers and college tutors who may have no experience of operational conditions.

A model of a competence-based training system is shown in Figure 5.1. As can be seen from the model, appraising people's performance is an important part of the training and development process. There are three good reasons for appraising people's performance. These are:

- to find out how effectively people's skills are being used
- to identify training needs to improve current performance
- to identify potential for promotion to more senior levels.

Performance appraisal is now a well-established part of normal business procedure, and there is a variety of appraisal methods available, which are outside the scope of this book. It is worthwhile, however, re-stating the most important aspects of the appraisal process. These are:

- Appraisal is concerned with how well the employee is doing the job and to be effective it must measure performance.
- Performance is concerned with measurable results.
- Results should be measurable against specific objectives – the employee must have a clear understanding of what he/she is expected to do and to what standard.
- People are encouraged to analyse and improve their own performance.

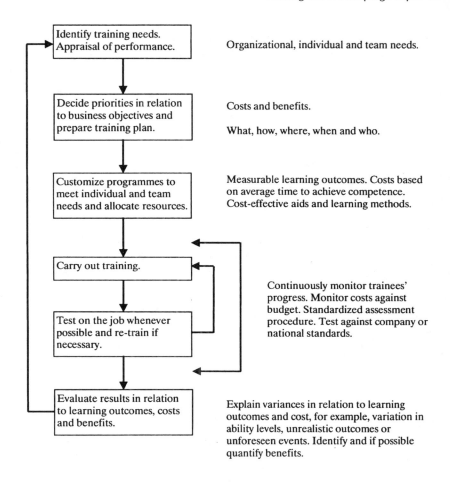

Figure 5.1 Competence-based training

▨ Training needs are identified which form the basis for customized training programmes to improve current performance.
▨ Potential for promotion is identified which forms the basis for a development programme.

Appraisal of performance is applicable to all areas of the business and at all levels. Other training needs arise as a result of change in business objectives, for example, the introduction of new technology, or the launching of a new product.

An ability to do the current job is no longer enough in a constantly changing business environment. People at work need to be adaptable and prepared to learn new skills and knowledge throughout their working life. The days when operators sat waiting at their machines for a maintenance fitter to arrive and sort out the problem are largely over. In WCOs people are trained to plan, do and finish off tasks; to recognize faults and take corrective action and to carry out simple routine maintenance of machines and equipment. Multi-skilling and teamwork is on the increase, as is the necessity to perform more than one job in order to cover in case of absence. The effective implementation of a customer-centred strategy requires people who can solve problems, use their initiative and manage themselves.

Another important aspect of an individual's job that WCOs are seeking to develop in their workforce is an awareness of the importance of fully satisfying internal and external customers' needs and expectations, their contribution to the achievement of business objectives and an understanding of the stages of the process leading to products and services, even when these may be remote to one's own part in the overall process. WCOs provide financial incentives for people to study in their own time and, in many cases, provide well-equipped learning centres where people can study during breaks or in out-of-work hours.

It is important that training and development programmes are based on measurable performance objectives, otherwise it is not possible to effectively validate or evaluate the training. Objectives should state what the individual will be able to do, to what standard and under what conditions: for example, operate a CNC lathe to company standards under normal operational conditions. Outcomes may also be stated in organizational terms. For example, the outcome of a training programme might be to reduce waste by 2 per cent by a target date or to commission new plant and equipment on time.

If competence-based training is to be implemented throughout the organization, consideration must be given to the manning levels required for training to take place. All too often senior managers say they are committed to training, but fail to provide sufficient resources for it to take place effectively. I have met many well-intentioned managers and supervisors who wanted to train their people, but were unable to do so because of insufficient manning to allow them to release their people for training. One way of minimizing this problem is to encourage self-study and training in out-of-work hours, preferably in company learning centres. If people know what they have to learn and to what standard, they can plan and organize much of their own learning, especially the knowledge and theory underpinning jobs.

Skills, whenever possible, should be acquired on the job under the supervision of an occupationally competent person, preferably trained in instructional and assessment techniques. Competence-testing procedures should be standardized and supported by assessment aids which specify criteria for successful performance: for example, competence checklists such as those used in the car driving test. It is also important to check related knowledge and understanding even though much of this may be inferred from the actual doing of the task. Time taken to achieve competence will, of course, vary according to ability, aptitude and learning opportunities.

An often neglected, but very important, aspect of competence-based training is evaluation. Senior management should review the effectiveness of their investment in people. Put simply, were the results of our training and development activities worthwhile? Were the costs outweighed by the benefits? What were the benefits and are they quantifiable? It is also important to evaluate whether or not people's newly acquired skills and knowledge are being put to good use.

Finally, it is important to remember that the primary objective of a company's training system is to ensure that there is an adequate supply of competent people to meet operational demands, change and contingencies at all levels within the company. It is also important to bear in mind that the training should be standards-based and cost-effective.

THE MANAGER AS COACH

Ideally, all trainers, managers and supervisors should be trained in coaching and assessment techniques, and for this purpose the well-established and effective five-step approach to coaching is suitable (see Figure 5.2).

Step 1 – Prepare to coach

- Identify learning opportunities.

  Operational problems, on-the-job tasks, faults, customer complaints.

- Prepare and gather together appropriate learning aids.

  Manuals, faults charts, task breakdowns, standard procedures, etc.

- Divide the coaching into logical steps and identify key points.

  Factors affecting quality, output, specification, speed of working, safety, customer satisfaction.

- Ensure that everything is ready and properly arranged before starting to coach.

  Saves time and creates a professional image.

Step 2 – Motivate learner

- Put the learner at ease.

  If people are not at ease they can't concentrate.

- State the job or task to be done and to what standard.

  If people know what they have to learn and to what standard, they can plan and organize their own learning.

- Create an interest in learning.

  People need to understand the importance of what they do in achieving business objectives and in meeting the needs of their internal or external customers.

Step 3 – Coach

- Tell, show, illustrate, as appropriate, in easily digestible steps.

  Don't underestimate learning difficulties. Familiarity breeds contempt. People cannot recall information if it is presented too quickly.

- Stress key points and explain reasons for actions.

Emphasize factors affecting output, quality, safety and speed of working. It is important that trainees understand the what, how and why.

Step 4 – Guidance and feedback on performance

- Observe trainee's performance.

- Correct errors as they occur.

To prevent bad habits from forming. Encourage trainees to find out what the error was themselves.

- Check understanding of key points.

Use questions to establish that trainee knows and understands key points and reasons for actions.

- Continue with practice until trainee knows and understands key points and is able to perform the task:

Time taken to master task will vary according to trainee's motivation, ability and progress.

  – correctly.
  – safely.

Step 5 – Practice under supervision

- Monitor and record trainee's progress and take corrective action as required.

A record of progress can help to motivate trainees and speed up the learning process.

- Continue with practice until trainee is able to perform task to company or national standards, that is:

  – correctly.

The procedure for certificating competence may be based on continuous assessment or an end test.

– safely.
– at an appropriate
    speed of working.

● Record trainee's   This should be kept by the trainee as
  achievements.   evidence of achievement.

Figure 5.2   The five-step approach to coaching

Coaching involves using work as an opportunity for planned learning. Coaching should be an integral part of every manager's role, from senior managers down to first line supervisors, but surprisingly it is often neglected. The effective coach takes every opportunity to develop people through work-based learning by giving them challenging but achievable tasks to perform or problems to solve, supported by guidance, feedback and regular review of performance. Learning opportunities abound at work. For example, taking people to meetings, getting people to act as chairman or discussion leader, giving people assignments or projects that tackle real work problems or placing people for training with employees who are occupationally competent and effective coaches.

An important coaching skill is the ability to provide both positive and negative feedback effectively. Negative feedback, given skillfully, can play an important part in helping to improve performance. Conversely destructive feedback leaves the person feeling demoralized and resentful and with nothing on which to build. Unfortunately, our culture tends to emphasize the negative with the focus on mistakes more often than strengths. Managers often overlook the things that have been done well. But it is important to remember that the object of feedback is to improve performance and morale. It does not make good sense, therefore, to end a feedback session with the other person feeling resentful and hurt. I know that it is not always possible to avoid this, but it is worth trying. Following negative feedback, therefore, an attempt should be made to end the session with a positive comment about the person or some aspect of their work.

COMPETENCE-BASED QUALIFICATIONS

In the past ten years, a quiet revolution has taken place which has radically changed the delivery, content and assessment procedures of industrial training and vocational qualifications in Britain. The reasons for the changes are complex and beyond the scope of this book, but it is important for managers and supervisors to understand what the potential benefits are to industry and commerce and some of the problems created by the new National Vocational Qualifications (NVQs) and General National Vocational Qualifications (GNVQs).

The primary distinction between NVQs and GNVQs is that NVQs set standards for the functions actually performed in employment, whereas GNVQs set standards for skills, knowledge and understanding within broad vocational areas, each of which underpin a range of NVQs. Thus, NVQs certificate occupational competence and GNVQs certificate achievement in a broad vocational area. Training and assessment for NVQs, especially at lower levels take place mainly in-company, whereas learning and assessment for GNVQs take place mainly in schools and colleges.

At the time of the creation of the National Council for Vocational Qualifications (NCVQ), there was a heated debate about the advantages and disadvantages of basing a national qualifications system on competence at work rather than on training standards (see Figure 5.3).

Opponents of competence-based qualifications argued that national standards should be based on a broad range of skills and knowledge underpinning competence in a broad occupational field, for example, retailing or engineering. Training, it was argued, based on skills, knowledge and principles gave trainees the understanding needed to cope with contingencies and change. Principles, it was claimed, remained valid when methods, technology, procedures and techniques changed. It was argued, that competence-based training at company level was sensible, effective and responsive to change, but was hardly a sound basis for the development of national standards.

Competence, it was argued, varied from company to company and even within the same firm different standards are sometimes found in different departments. Additionally, standards of competence are changing so rapidly that to base national standards on them is a bit like

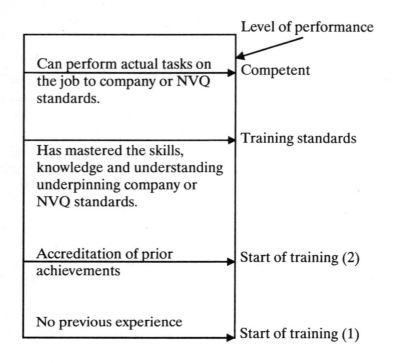

Figure 5.3 Competence and training standards

building a house on shifting sand. The only sensible way, critics said, to define national standards would be to base qualifications on training standards, that is the skills, knowledge and understanding underpinning a broad range of tasks at work, rather than competence at work. This approach, it was argued, would facilitate national training programmes of common content and standardized assessment procedures which could be quickly up-dated to meet change.

Despite the strong arguments against competence-based qualifications, it was decided to go ahead with their development and the NCVQ set itself three objectives: first, to rationalize and simplify the provision of vocational qualifications; second, to facilitate progression; and, third, to make provision comprehensive, covering all significant occupations and work activities. Initially, it was decided to develop four levels of competence covering basic operator skills to higher level technical and managerial skills. The number has now been extended to include management and professional qualifications.

Despite early teething problems, there is growing evidence to show that NVQs, especially at lower levels, offer significant benefits for companies and people at work. For example:

- Employees can gain recognition for previously acquired skills, knowledge and understanding through a process known as 'accreditation of prior learning'.
- Training is flexible since units of competence can be selected to meet individual requirements.
- Employees can learn and gain credit for new units to meet change.
- Company-specific units can be added to NVQ units to ensure that local needs are fully met.
- Since learning and assessment can take place at work, training is more relevant and cost-effective than traditional training leading to qualifications.
- Confidence of customers in a company's products or services is often influenced by the way they perceive the competence and qualifications of its people.
- Companies can pick-and-mix units of competence to create customized training programmes.
- NVQs are standards to be achieved and do not prescribe any particular learning route or learning method. That is, the standards can be achieved in a variety of ways and means.
- NVQs allow certification at the end of in-company training which can be motivating for trainees.

NVQs and GNVQs are gradually replacing traditional qualifications and at the end of 1992 some 80 per cent of roles below professional level were covered by NVQs. A national database of vocational qualifications is also available which contains information on all NVQs, including the units of competence that appear in each one and full details of their elements, range statements and performance criteria. The information is updated at regular intervals and is available on subscription. A measure of the impact that NVQs are having on training and education is shown by the fact that at the end of June 1993 the number of NVQ certificates awarded was 379,446.

Of special interest to managers and supervisors are the management standards produced by the Management Charter Initiative (MCI). These standards are being used to produce a broad range of management and supervisory competence-based qualifications at all levels, including qualifications for trainers and assessors of NVQs. The MCI Standards are available from the Management Charter Initiative, Russell Square House, 10–12 Russell Square, London WC1B 5BZ.

Despite the claimed benefits, there are still many problems to be overcome, especially the jargon associated with NVQs, the problems of interpreting performance criteria and range statements and the bureaucracy of the verification process needed to confirm that assessment procedures are valid and reliable. There is also a danger of too much emphasis being given to skills as opposed to theory. We are entering the age of the knowledge-based society and our vocational qualifications should reflect that fact, especially GNVQs.

In response to considerable criticism of standards and assessment procedures, NVQs are to undergo substantial (March 1995) revision to improve the quality and rigour of the system. Reacting to the demands of employers, NVQs will have increased flexibility, with mandatory 'core skills' units plus options. They will also include specifications for essential knowledge and understanding underpinning skills at work. Regional centres are to be established with NCVQ field staff providing local quality monitoring. These measures, it is hoped, will make the assessment process more consistent and less open to abuse, re-establish the credibility of NVQs and encourage increased take-up of the qualifications.

As Britain seeks to compete effectively in a demanding world market, competence-related vocational qualifications will play an increasingly important role in our education and training system. It is important that such qualifications are: meeting the needs of employers, flexible, credible, widely understood, readily available and vigorously marketed.

One of the primary aims of senior management should be to establish a 'learning organization' that aims to provide an adequate supply of competent and flexible people at all levels within the organization. A competent and adaptable workforce is an essential part of the drive to improve performance, customer satisfaction and business results. This fact is reflected in the increasing emphasis being given to investment in people. Other things being equal, a competent and adaptable workforce can give a company a competitive edge.

So how does your organization measure up? Complete the profile below and find out.

Performance Improvement Criteria
Training and Developing People

For completion by senior management

Appraisal criteria	Appraisal rating
	5 = Fully agree with criterion
	1 = Strongly disagree with the criterion/don't know

All our people are aware of the company's commitment to training and development.

5 4 3 2 1

When we take decisions about the future, we consider the training implications for people at the same time and give them the opportunity to comment before we finalize our plans.

5 4 3 2 1

We have a recruitment policy, standardized recruitment procedures and valid and reliable recruitment tests which are administered by trained people.

5 4 3 2 1

Senior managers regularly visit training events and involve themselves in training activities.

5 4 3 2 1

Senior management demonstrate their commitment to developing people by their actions in providing the opportunity for people to develop themselves (time, money, resources).

5 4 3 2 1

▓ All management are held accountable
for their training responsibilities,
including the identification of training needs
and the planning, implementation and
evaluation of training.   5 4 3 2 1

▓ All employees are provided with the
training and development they need
to cope with entry to the firm, their
current job, flexibility and change.   5 4 3 2 1

▓ Training programmes are customized to meet
the identified needs of the organization,
teams and individuals.   5 4 3 2 1

▓ Training is regularly reviewed and
evaluated in relation to the relevance
of learning objectives, costs and
benefits.   5 4 3 2 1

▓ The firm has a good reputation
amongst its employees as a provider
of good quality training and
development.   5 4 3 2 1

▓ The proportion of our employees with
a vocational qualification is equal to
or greater than that of our main
competitors.   5 4 3 2 1

▓ We have identified organizations that
we could use for benchmarking purposes.   5 4 3 2 1

Interpretation of results

50 to 60   Well on the way to establishing a 'learning
                organization', standard on a par with the
                Investor in People national standard.

40 to 49   Significant development need.

Less than 40   Major development need.

UK firms scoring 50+ should consider applying for the Investor in People award (IIP). For further information on the IIP award contact your local Training and Enterprise Council.

6

Management of resources

PRODUCTIVITY

Productivity is typically the driving force when firms compete on the
basis of efficiency and cost with much emphasis on the financial side.
The productivity of a process is a measure of the ratio between the
output of the process and the input of the resources, that is:

$$\text{Productivity} = \frac{\text{Output}}{\text{Input}}$$

Examples of productivity measures include output per man hour,
output per machine hour, output per pound of input and output per
material unit. The most commonly used measure of productivity is
manpower. However, in many firms manpower is a relatively low
component of the total cost of a product or service. It is often mislead-
ing, therefore, to quote productivity performance solely on manpower
and it is important to consider all resource inputs to give the total
resource productivity. In this case, all inputs are converted into monetary values and divided into the output to establish the output per
pound of input.

Two factors affecting productivity are utilization and efficiency. Utilization refers to the degree to which the resources committed to a process are actually converted into a product or service. Efficiency is concerned with the speed and accuracy with which the conversion is accomplished. Clearly then, productivity can be increased by increasing the utilization of people, machines and materials or by improving efficiency; for example, reducing cycle times and waste. However, it is important to remember that improvement in productivity requires the optimal use of all resources – manpower, machinery, materials and money.

The cost of any product or service is the sum of the costs of the resources used in producing it. One way, therefore, of increasing productivity is to lower the costs of the resources used, including manpower. But for many firms it may not be a realistic option to cut wages in order to compete. Increasingly, therefore, firms have been seeking other ways to increase productivity and in recent years there has been a growing realization that one of the most effective ways to increase productivity is by reducing cycle times and waste (see Chapter 7). Technology is also making a major impact on both productivity and flexibility.

USING TECHNOLOGY TO IMPROVE PRODUCTIVITY AND FLEXIBILITY

Customer satisfaction, productivity and flexibility are at the heart of the competitive battle. In the past ten years particular emphasis has been given to improving customer satisfaction and productivity – led by Japanese companies. However, flexibility – for example, lead times, on-time delivery for rush orders, concept to market time and the number of products using common processes – is now being touted as the next competitive battle and there is ample evidence to show that the Japanese, in particular, are concentrating on improving their ability to respond quickly to change in customer requirements. Just-in-time (JIT) techniques, for example, are drastically reducing throughput time and computer-integrated manufacturing is allowing rapid changeover for increased responsiveness.

JIT techniques can substantially reduce cycle times: for example, build computers in days, replenish supermarket shelves within hours and make and deliver car components in minutes; JIT relies heavily on information technology to create real-time links through the customer/supplier chain. JIT is not simply a matter of making suppliers further down the line hold stock you do not yet need, it is also about eliminating wastage within all processes of the organization. In other words, JIT is not just about external suppliers.

JIT methods are beginning to alter the relationship between customers and external suppliers. Partnership arrangements based on mutual cooperation and trust are being developed. Some organizations are forming close relationships with their suppliers to ensure consistent quality and on-time delivery which can drastically reduce costs and increase flexibility leading to greater customer satisfaction. For JIT companies the days when minimum cost was the main criterion for selecting suppliers are over. Companies now help their suppliers to control their processes to improve quality and reduce costs and to introduce and use the technology needed to operate a JIT system effectively. With the help of computers and sophisticated information systems linking customers, wholesalers and suppliers and the various production stages within the factory together, it is possible to reduce stocks by astonishing levels.

Properly applied, technology can dramatically improve performance and reduce costs: for example, the use of EDI – electronic data interchange – for automating transactions between organizations. EDI enables orders, acknowledgements and invoices to be transmitted between customers' and suppliers' computers anywhere in the world without any exchange of paperwork. EDI speeds up the flow of information between buyer and supplier, enabling the supplier to provide a better service; it enables the supplier to streamline administration and cut costs and it removes the constraints of geography – an order can be sent anywhere in the world in seconds.

An important development has been the introduction of computer networking within and between companies. This makes it possible to separate tasks geographically while integrating them electronically, so that companies can relocate functions to far-flung countries if need be and still maintain control. It allows managers to keep tabs on workers through real-time information like the insurance companies, for example, which pay clerical staff according to the number of times they strike the keyboard. It also overcomes the administrative barriers erected by bureaucracy, since managers can bypass them to get information direct.

A good example of the impact of technology on productivity is the use of document image processing (DIP) which protects documents from accidental loss, disclosure and misfiling and provides rapid retrieval facilities to approved users. Productivity gains of 30–40 per cent on basic document retrieval applications and over 100 per cent in more complex cases have been achieved (source: *A Guide to Workflow and Business Re-engineering* – Olivetti).

An important development in the use of technology is workflow computing which automates the flow of information to support the flow of work. At each stage the user is provided with all the information needed to complete the work and given guidance on how to proceed to the next stage. Workflow systems are most successful when used to support re-engineered business processes (see Chapter 7), as they ensure that the right work is carried out at the right time automatically. Because the way in which the work is done is defined, managers can monitor and control the productivity of the group and measure and check the quality of the work all members of the team produce.

Computers are the factories and warehouses of the 1990s. They play the same role in the information society as factories and warehouses played in the 1940s and 1950s. But unlike equipment stored in a warehouse, computers cannot only store information, they can also manipulate it and turn it into new information that can be used for decision-making purposes and to increase competitiveness. Virtually all walks of business life are being affected by the information technology revolution and it will become increasingly difficult for firms to compete unless they are prepared to invest in technology and in the people who will be expected to make it work effectively.

FINANCIAL RESOURCES

Two vitally important financial measures are profitability and working capital. There are three fundamental ways to increase profit: you can reduce your fixed and variable costs, raise your selling price or increase sales turnover.

It's all too easy to fall into the trap of reducing prices to try and increase sales at a time of recession and difficult trading times. This course of action could be counter-productive, however, since you then have to work a lot harder for less return. For example, if a company has a gross profit margin of 30 per cent and decides to reduce the selling price by 15 per cent, it would have to generate 100 per cent more sales to compensate for the price reduction! Conversely, if the company decides to increase prices by 10 per cent, it could afford to lose 25 per cent sales volume. Not surprisingly, some businesses get sucked into a spiral of decline and failure during difficult times because they cut prices, believing that they have to maintain turnover at all costs. By asking some basic questions this unfortunate fate could, in many cases, be avoided. For example:

- How many extra sales do we need to generate to maintain profits if we lower selling prices by 5 per cent, 10 per cent and so on.
- What sales do we need to generate to maintain profits if we raise prices by 5 per cent, 10 per cent and so on.

As obvious as this may seem, in my experience, it often is not done and companies end up cutting prices when in some cases it would be more effective to raise prices.

Cash and profit are not the same. Managing your cash effectively is about making sure you receive money owed to you before you spend it. Cash can mean survival and companies should have a long-term and short-term cash flow forecast which will help them to identify danger areas and where cuts should be made. A credit control system is also important in enabling companies to ensure that they do not run out of cash. Profitability comes from running your business effectively, making sure that your pricing is right and controlling costs.

Many companies found in the 1989–1992 recession that the key to survival was effective control of costs and margins. But to retain control requires an information system that enables you to make sensible judgements about, for example:

▓ pricing your goods and services at the right level for the market (profit margin)
▓ whether you are breaking even or not
▓ your cash flow.

MONITORING PERFORMANCE

All managers should have an understanding of the key ratios used to monitor business operations such as liquidity ratios, solvency ratios and efficiency ratios. These are outside the scope of this book but the following point should be borne in mind – cash is survival, so keep your working capital up. This is especially the case for small companies. In the long term a business cannot survive unless it makes profits. In the short term it cannot survive if it does not generate sufficient cash to pay daily cash outgoings. Monitoring cashflow is, therefore, vital and two important ratios are:

$$\text{Current ratio} = \frac{\text{Current assets}}{\text{Current liabilities}}$$

This ratio is also known as the working capital ratio. This should normally be between 1.5 and 2. An upward trend indicates that the business is tying up an increasing amount of cash in working capital. If it falls below 1, that is, current liabilities are more than current assets, urgent action may be needed to correct the situation. Conversely, if the ratio is over 2 you should check that you are effectively using your cash, especially in regard to stock and debtors. However, it is important to realize that money tied up in current assets could be better used to improve the efficiency of the business, so many companies nowadays keep the ratio as low as possible commensurate with the risk involved. They do this by using up stocks more rapidly, keeping stocks to a minimum by using JIT and expediting payments from debtors.

Most importantly you need to know how long the business can survive if no more cash flows into it. This is usually called the defensive interval (DI) and varies according to the type of industry. It is usually between 30 to 90 days. The DI is given by the so-called 'quick assets' – that is, current assets minus, for example, stock and work in progress which it might be hard to sell quickly – divided by the daily operating expenses:

$$\text{Defensive interval} = \frac{\text{Quick assets}}{\text{Daily operating expenses}}$$

Remember, many potentially successful companies have failed because they neglected to manage and monitor their cashflow. The following important points should be borne in mind:

- Use ratios to examine trends and to identify problems and their causes.
- The smaller the business, the more important it is to watch cashflow, rather than just the ratios.
- An information system that is reliable, consistent and up to date is essential if ratios are to be used effectively.
- If you rely too heavily on borrowed money (interest rates may suddenly rise, sales may drop whilst margins deteriorate, costs may not be able to be brought down rapidly), the consequences could be disaster!
- Cash is survival, so keep your working capital up.

Performance Improvement Criteria
Management of Resources

For completion by managers with appropriate knowledge and expertise

Appraisal criteria	Appraisal rating
	5 = Strongly agree
	1 = Strongly disagree/don't know

Note: some criteria require a yes or no answer, ie 5 or 1 score

Financial resources:

- Have you done a long- and short-term
  cash flow analysis?   **5 4 3 2 1**

- Do you have a credit control system?   **5 4 3 2 1**

▓ Have you identified key financial control
ratios?   5 4 3 2 1

▓ Have you identified organizations which
you could use for benchmarking purposes?   5 4 3 2 1

Information resources

▓ Does your information system provide
managers with the information they
need, when they need it and in an
easy-to-understand format?   5 4 3 2 1

▓ Do you know:
  – how your information systems compare
    with those of your competitors?   5 4 3 2 1
  – which organizations could be used for
    benchmarking purposes?   5 4 3 2 1

▓ Do you regularly review your information
systems with a view to improving:
  – collection of information?   5 4 3 2 1
  – analysis of information?   5 4 3 2 1
  – scope and relevance of information?   5 4 3 2 1
  – availability and presentation of
    information?   5 4 3 2 1
  – dissemination of information?   5 4 3 2 1
  – Are suppliers, internal and external
    customers involved in the review?   5 4 3 2 1

Application of technology

▓ Have you evaluated how you can use
technology to give you a competitive
edge?   5 4 3 2 1

▓ Do you compare your use of technology
with that of your main competitors in
relation to:
  – stock control?   5 4 3 2 1

– production control?   **5 4 3 2 1**
– financial control?   **5 4 3 2 1**
– design?   **5 4 3 2 1**

▨ Have you identified which organizations
   you could use for benchmarking purposes
   in relation to:
– application of technology?   **5 4 3 2 1**
– utilization of resources?   **5 4 3 2 1**

▨ Do you regularly review how effectively you
   use technology and resources?   **5 4 3 2 1**

Measuring, Monitoring and Improving Productivity

▨ Do you have a system for measuring
   and monitoring the productivity of:
– manpower?   **5 4 3 2 1**
– machinery?   **5 4 3 2 1**
– materials?   **5 4 3 2 1**
– money?   **5 4 3 2 1**

▨ Have you identified the best performers for
   benchmarking?   **5 4 3 2 1**

▨ Do you regularly review and up-date
   your performance measures?   **5 4 3 2 1**

Interpretation of results

120 to 135   Effective management of resources.

100 to 119   Significant development need.

less than 100   Major development need.

7

Process control and improvement

Performance measure '6'

Productivity, unit costs and flexibility are as good as, or better than, the best of the competition.

INTERNAL AND EXTERNAL CUSTOMERS

In every organization there are many internal customers and suppliers and many interfaces between departments and functions (see Figure 7.1). It is hardly surprising, therefore, that processing mistakes are a major cause of customer dissatisfaction. According to the Department of Trade and Industry in its publication *Total Quality Management and Effective Leadership*, failing to satisfy customers' needs and expectations, or failing to do so right first time, costs the average company between 15 and 30 per cent of sales revenue and it costs the average service organization up to 40 per cent of budget, an appalling waste.

Many products pass through a number of external and internal customers and suppliers and a multiplicity of processes. A good example of this is the manufacture of sheet steel to a specification set by the car manufacturers. Before reaching the end of the manufacturing process, sheet steel has to pass through many processes, some of which are shown in Figure 7.1. At each of these stages, there are suppliers and customers and critical input, process and output measures: for example, raw material specification, chemical composition of the iron and steel, casting temperature, hot rolling and finishing temperatures, gauge, and surface quality. All these intermediate specifications must be met to ensure that the final product meets the specification of the external customer.

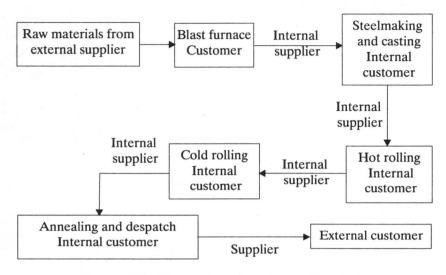

Figure 7.1 The customer and supplier chain

It is not surprising, therefore, that most problems arise where there are handovers between one supplier and a customer and especially between functions or departments, owing to poor communication, unclear responsibilities, lack of knowledge about the internal customer's exact requirements or a failure to control and monitor the process. How often do you get error-free work back from the typing pool, set out as you want it, on time? Typists (suppliers) need to know their customers' requirements and, conversely, customers need to know what the typist needs – legible handwriting, clear instructions, and so on.

To avoid costly mistakes, each person in the customer/supplier chain must:

▓ know what they are expected to do, how to do it and to what standard (standard operating instructions)

▓ perform their tasks right first time

▓ obtain immediate feedback when things go wrong.

Standardization and control improves productivity by reducing waste and the time spent on re-work, inspection and customer complaints. A major task, therefore, is to ensure that processes are customized and brought under control so that consistent products and services are produced every time.

Unfortunately, internal supplier/customer requirements are often poorly defined and based on the assumption that people up or down the chain know what the requirements are. But this is often not the case, and waste, errors and delays result which eventually manifest themselves in a failure to fully satisfy external customers' requirements. Important questions to be addressed by customers include:

▓ Who are my suppliers – internal and external?

▓ Do they know exactly what my requirements are?

▓ Do I keep them fully informed of changes in my requirements?

▓ Do I provide them with immediate feedback when things go wrong?

▓ Are my suppliers' processes customized and under control (for example, BS EN ISO 9000)?

Important questions to be addressed by suppliers include:

▓ Who are my customers – internal and external?

▓ Do I know exactly what they require of me?

▓ Do I have performance measures to assess how effectively I am meeting my customers' needs?

▓ Are my processes under control?

▓ Have all my people been trained to do their tasks right every time?

CUSTOMIZATION AND CONTROL OF PROCESSES

A process is the transformation of a set of inputs into desired outputs (see Figure 7.2). Customization is the process of finding out exactly what internal and external customers' needs are and then designing or re-designing processes to meet those requirements, that is, designing quality in, rather than inspecting faults out. Consistency of outcome can only be achieved if the same inputs are used in the conversion process in the same way every time. The process is then said to be under control. That doesn't mean, however, that it cannot be improved and WCOs strive to ensure that their processes, work methods and use of technology are as good as, or better than, the best in the sector. Their ultimate aim is to achieve world class standards through a process of continuous improvement.

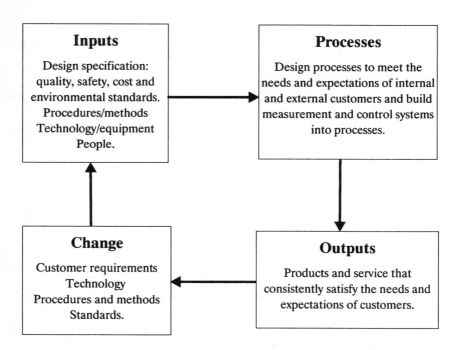

Figure 7.2 Customization and control of processes

I first became convinced of the benefits of process control, benchmarking, customized competence-based training, self-managed project teams and the contribution that shop floor employees could make to the solution of business problems in the 1960s when, because of my background in quality control and training, I was asked to join a multi-discipline project team (led by Bill Morgan) to help commission a new high-technology galvanizing line at the British Steel Corporation's Ebbw Vale plant. The team comprised a metallurgist, a mechanical engineer, an electrical engineer, two training officers, craftsmen and senior operatives.

The objectives of the project were to commission a new high-technology process line 2 on time without adversely affecting production on an older existing process line 1. The only other line 2 in existence was in America which meant there was no plant close by that could be used for training purposes. A further complication was the decision to transfer 50 per cent of operatives from line 1 to line 2 and make up the balance on both lines with 'green' labour.

A critical path analysis was conducted and this formed the basis of an action plan which, apart from some minor exceptions, was successfully implemented. Analysis of the operating procedures of the three shifts working on line 1 revealed significant differences in methods of work and job operating procedures. It was subsequently established that these variations in procedure were a major cause of the significant differences in the performance of the three teams. Standard operating procedures based on best practice were, therefore, agreed and established on line 1.

At the same time, the project team held a number of brainstorming meetings in order to generate information and ideas that could be used for training people on line 2. This process resulted in questionnaires covering mechanical, electrical, quality, and operating issues. These questionnaires were used by project team members who went to America to observe the only other line 2 in operation at that time. On their return they were debriefed and the information was used by the team to develop learning materials, faults analysis charts and standard operating procedures based on best-known practice at that time.

Each of the project team members were trained in instructional techniques (see the five-step approach to coaching, Figure 5.2). They were also involved in the preparation and writing of customized training programmes, learning materials and standard operating procedures which they used for off-the-job training sessions and, as plant and equipment became available, to provide on-the-job instruction. Both objectives were achieved – line 2 was commissioned on time and planned production targets met. At the same time output was maintained on line 1 during the transfer, recruitment, and training of people for both lines.

When customizing processes, it is important to start at the point where the first supplier provides input into the process and continue through to the point at which the external customer is supplied with the output. The aim is to move progressively to a position where all processes are under control and all inputs are always capable of meeting the requirements of the process. The process should then be able to deliver products and services that fully meet customers' requirements first time.

A word of caution, however. Some service and especially 'knowhow' organizations are engaged in much more complex, less standardized tasks and problem solving than industrial companies – for example a lawyer, doctor, lecturer or R&D worker. In these cases, tasks are often unstructured and it is not always possible to get it right first time – indeed, there may not be just one right way or solution. Nevertheless, this does not invalidate the wisdom of structuring tasks and systems which lend themselves to this approach. For example, most bank employees now supply relatively standardized services and only a small minority deal with client-oriented activities requiring higher levels of skill. Another move in the direction of standardization is the development of so-called 'expert systems'. Increasingly, the move is towards speed, accuracy and replication of standardized products and services.

To control a process requires standardized procedures and performance measures which can be used to monitor and control processes so that immediate corrective action can be taken when things go wrong. Typical process performance measures include:

▓ **Quality –**	Does the process consistently deliver goods and services that meet internal and external customers' requirements?
▓ **Delivery –**	Does the process deliver goods and services on time, every time?
▓ **Cycle times –**	Are cycle times as good as or better than main competitors? For example, time to market, development time, manufacturing lead time, department throughput time, order processing time, batch processing time.

░ **Waste –**   Are waste rates as good as or better than main competitors? For example, cost of rejected materials, rework, in-process scrap, in-coming inspection, warranty costs.

For measurement to be effective, it must be relevant, it must be current and not historic, and it must be on the process and not at the end of it, which may be too late. Thus, measurement points should be as close as possible to known causes of problems or faults: for example, spellcheck programmes which provide immediate feedback and correction of errors. Similarly, statistical process control (SPC) techniques provide immediate feedback when a process moves outside an upper or lower limit.

. The aim should be to build the feedback system into the process, rather than to inspect faults at the end or after a customer has complained. Final inspection will not improve the quality of the internal processes or of the final product or service, it will just reduce the chances of a defective product getting through to the customer.

RE-ENGINEERING

In the 1970s and 1980s customer responsiveness and productivity were at the heart of the competitive battle and the Japanese strategy of total quality, process control, continuous improvement and effective use of technology was amazingly successful. There are signs, however, that other nations are mounting a counter-attack which threaten to undermine Japan's market dominance. For example, in North and South America, parts of South-east Asia and the United Kingdom, business re-engineering is leading to 'quantum leap' improvements in performance and transforming the fortunes of once-ailing companies.

Re-engineering is not about continuously improving processes and jobs to make incremental improvements in performance. It is about challenging the fundamental assumptions that underlie operations and then re-designing them to meet or exceed customer expectations. In other words, it means going back to the drawing board and starting all over again. Instead of looking at a business as a cluster of vertical functions – for example, design, production and marketing – re-engineering sees an organization as a cluster of horizontal processes that provide a service or product to an internal or external customer. Each process starts at the initial order or enquiry, passes through a number of process stages, and ends with delivery of the product or service to the customer.

Re-engineering aims to dismantle the barriers that cause costly delays between functions and re-focus the organization to serve the needs of customers. All too often functionally-based organizations become overmanned and unresponsive to the customer. People work in little boxes and are more concerned with maintaining their status and defending their patches than with serving customers. I have experienced this myself in a number of organizations overburdened with bureaucrats and planners who were experts in what I call 'armchair theorizing' and generating discussion papers and reports that aimed to strengthen their role, protect their patch and justify the status quo. They were able to do this because of the complexity of the organization and the fact that they were safe and remote from the critical eye of the customer they were supposed to be serving. It is hardly surprising, therefore, that these people resist change designed to serve the needs and expectations of their customers.

The Japanese are responding to recession by raising their competitiveness still further. They are doing this, not through quantum leap re-engineering, but by maintaining their traditional commitment to continuous improvement on every front – for example, in time taken to market new products, in the speed of manufacture and delivery, in stock turn rates and in cost and total productivity. This strategy is effective because most Japanese firms start from a higher level of efficiency and effectiveness than their Western rivals.

Nevertheless, re-engineering makes sense in an increasingly unstructured environment – when customer needs and expectations change, processes must also change. There comes a time when incremental improvements are no longer effective and the only answer is to go back to the drawing board and start all over again. In today's highly competitive and rapidly changing climate, businesses will probably need to re-engineer their operational processes every five years or sooner.

Despite notable successes, re-engineering is not an easy option and is beset with difficulties: for example, a failure to effectively manage the change process; resistance from middle managers who often have most to lose because of the fewer management layers needed. Additionally, in larger organizations, re-engineering often involves massive job losses which makes it a difficult option for European firms which have to take account of the social impact of a re-engineering strategy. Nevertheless, as we move towards the 21st century, more and more firms will be forced by necessity to either re-engineer or go bust.

PERFORMANCE IMPROVEMENT TEAMS

Many companies employ teams to generate innovative ideas, solve problems and improve working practices. The composition, organization and control of these teams vary from ad hoc teams formed to tackle specific problems to small work groups that meet on a regular basis, such as performance improvement teams (PITs). In my experience, PITs work best when membership is voluntary – people are most committed to decisions they make themselves. The primary responsibility of PITs is to continuously seek ways and means of improving performance in their area of responsibility. Companywide incremental improvements can achieve significant improvements in performance.

When tackling complex unstructured problems, teams are often formed with a mix of skills that are relevant to the aims and objectives of the exercise. Such groups are often called working parties or project teams and people are normally invited to join these groups on the basis of their expertise. Such teams are often used to tackle problems associated with, for example, the installation of new plant, the commissioning of new technology or to tackle specific business problems. A project team might, for example, be commissioned to investigate and report on whether or not a process has reached the end of its life cycle. If there is little or no scope for further improvement, then re-engineering may be the only way to remain competitive – if a process works, improve it; if it doesn't work, re-design it.

The complexity of many processes and problems is beyond the control or expertise of any one individual and the use of cross-functional teams to tackle problems has many advantages, for example:

▨ The team reflects a range of experiences and opinions.

▨ Supporting evidence can be drawn from a range of sources.

▨ A variety of problems may be tackled, which are beyond the capability of any one individual.

▨ The problems are exposed to a greater diversity of knowledge, skill and experience.

▨ Cross-functional boundaries can be dealt with more easily.

▨ Teamwork creates a climate where everyone is required to contribute.

▨ The recommendations are likely to carry more weight than individual suggestions.

▨ There is likely to be greater commitment to solutions and recommendations.

It is important that PITs adopt a questioning approach and provide evidence to support their recommendations to senior management. Key questions include:

▨ What are we doing and why are we doing it this way?

▨ Are we doing it as well as our main competitors?

▨ What are the causes of poor performance or exceptionally good performance? What evidence is there to support our findings?

▨ What action should be taken to standardize best practice and disseminate it throughout the organization?

▨ What are the options for eliminating the causes of poor performance?

▨ What are the cost and resource implications of each option?

▨ Which option is likely to give best value for money?

▨ What evidence do we need to convince senior management of our findings?

BENCHMARKING

A powerful performance improvement technique which is widely practised by WCOs is benchmarking. No company should be too proud to learn from the good practices of other organizations. A detailed description of the benchmarking technique is beyond the scope of this book but, in general, it involves finding out which companies are world leaders in particular operations or techniques, for example, just in time (JIT), analysing what they do well and how they do it and then applying it with modifications to your own organization. Properly done it can lead to remarkable improvements in performance.

Benchmarking is, however, fraught with difficulties, for example, the fear of industrial espionage which stops many companies from releasing competitively sensitive information about their operations and techniques. One answer to this problem is to use the PIMS (profit impact of market strategy) data base which contains business information from more than 3000 companies. This huge volume of facts and figures enables organizations to compare themselves with the best in the world and highlight problem areas. Business information and industry characteristics are fed in, and within half an hour they will have been analysed and matched up with a league table of 'strategic peers'. The system can show you at a glance how you have fared compared with the best and the worst in your class in more than 30 measures of business performance. PIMS doesn't give you all the answers but it can help you to identify problem areas that need to be addressed if your company is to compete with the best.

Most companies would be more than satisfied to be number one in their particular class of competition. Quality improvement, however, is a never-ending process and Nissan, for example, has set a goal (called NX 96) of becoming the number one of all companies in Europe – an ambitious goal indeed. To do this they have identified certain areas where they realize they need to improve and developed a companywide plan to achieve their stated aim.

Performance Improvement Criteria
Control and Continuous Improvement of Processes

For completion by managers with appropriate knowledge and expertise

Appraisal criteria	Appraisal rating
	Maximum rating = Strongly agree
	1 = Strongly disagree

Note: some questions require a yes or no answer, ie 5 or 1 score

All key processes have been identified.   **5 4 3 2 1**

All key processes have been customized and
brought under control.   **5 4 3 2 1**

Major suppliers' processes have been
customized and brought under control.   **5 4 3 2 1**

Regular quality audits (at least annually)
are conducted.   **5 4 3 2 1**

Written standardized work procedures have
been prepared and are strictly enforced.   **5 4 3 2 1**

People have been trained to carry out their
tasks to standard.   **5 4 3 2 1**

Performance improvement teams have been
formed and given the information, tools,
training and empowerment they need to do
the job effectively.   **5 4 3 2 1**

Organizations have been identified
which could be used for benchmarking.   **5 4 3 2 1**

Managers encourage and support their
people to use their initiative and seek
ways of improving performance.   **5 4 3 2 1**

Exceptional performance is recognized and
rewarded.   **5 4 3 2 1**

Systems, methods and procedures are
regularly reviewed and up-dated in line with
best current practice.   **5 4 3 2 1**

Interpretation of results

50 to 55	Process control and improvement is on a par with the best of the competition.
35 to 49	Significant development need.
Less than 35	Major development need.

8

Customer satisfaction

Performance measure '7'

Customers rate the quality of products and services highly in relation to those of major competitors.

CUSTOMER SATISFACTION

Satisfied and loyal customers are major factors in the long-term success of an organization. It is important, therefore, to keep close to customers, listen to what they have to say and act on the information. The way a company handles customers' complaints can have a significant influence on customers' perceptions and a badly handled complaint can do considerable damage to a company's reputation. Not only will that customer not buy from you again, but he or she is likely to spread the word about how they were treated. Conversely, a satisfied customer becomes a powerful means of creating a positive company image.

The importance of creating positive customer perceptions is illustrated by the fact that a number of car manufacturers are still suffering from a reputation gained in the 1960s and 1970s that their cars are prone to rust. Although this is no longer the case, many consumers are still influenced by it. This demonstrates how difficult it is to change well-established customers' perceptions. According to Tom Peters, drawing on research from the PIMS data base (profit impact of market strategy), market share comes primarily through leadership in 'relative perceived product or service quality', where 'relative' means in relation to competitors and 'perceived' means as seen through the eyes of the customer. Changes in relative perceived product quality have a far more potent effect on market share than do changes in price.

The growth and continuing development of communications technology enables companies to deal with customer complaints far more quickly than before. For example, British Steel's advisory engineers who deal with customers are now equipped with a 'travelling office' comprising a laptop, printer, portable phone, fax and integral power supplies. This means that customer complaints can be dealt with on the spot with the customer, and reports sent directly to the supplying works using the fax link. Further developments will allow direct entry of complaints into the computer mainframe from the advisory engineer's work station. This will immediately process customer complaints with a further improvement in time to settlement.

To minimize costly errors, companies should have a companywide complaints policy that is easy to understand, widely disseminated and strictly enforced. The policy should specify what to do when a complaint is received, who is to deal with it and procedures to be followed, including the recording, categorization and analysis of all complaints. Every complaint successfully handled is likely to reinforce the image of the company as one that cares about its customers. Nothing is more irritating, for example, than a company that fails to call you back when they said they would or passes you from one person to another. Training, supported by standardized procedures, can help to avoid these pitfalls.

Particularly important are direct and indirect points of contact with customers. All too frequently, the image of a company is tarnished by an incompetent switchboard operator or receptionist using an inappropriate tone of voice, showing a lack of concern, adopting a take it or leave it attitude or displaying an uncertain and unprofessional manner. It is very important, therefore, to identify customer contact points and establish:

▒ what constitutes good performance – are actions leading to customer satisfaction?

▓ what constitutes poor performance – are actions leading to customer dissatisfaction?

Every customer contact provides an opportunity to improve the image of the company and increase sales. Of particular importance, therefore, is the selection and training of those people who have direct or indirect contact with external customers. Companies which are in the process of improving their responsiveness to customers have already discovered that, whilst it is in part about developing flexible systems and re-organizing operations, what really matters are the people who make the systems and procedures work and who are able to interact positively with customers.

What many customers, including myself, find frustrating are the woeful inadequacies of many of the instruction manuals that accompany some products. Assembly, start-up and operational procedures are often complex, full of technical jargon and quite unsuitable for a non-technical person to cope with. The customer is often forced to adopt a trial and error process. This is especially the case when setting up computers, fax machines, television sets and video recorders. Is it too much to expect companies to produce easy-to-follow step-by-step procedures written in plain English? After all, having spent millions of pounds developing a quality product, it seems a great shame that customers are then antagonized by the poor quality of the instruction manual. It doesn't help much either when sales people who are approached for advice often know less about the product than the customer. How many sales, I wonder, are lost because of sales assistants' lack of product knowledge?

Demands from consumers for quality products and services, including clear and concise operating instructions, on-site technical support and, if necessary, training, are likely to increase dramatically as we approach 2000 and companies should be asking themselves now:

▓ Are we devoting sufficient resources to the handling and analysis of customer complaints?
▓ Are our complaints procedures easy to understand and implement?
▓ Do we need to provide our staff with more customer service and product knowledge training?

▓ Are our technical support systems and procedures as good as those of our main competitors?

▓ Are our product users' manuals as good as, or better than, those of our main competitors?

Specific actions that can be taken by companies to improve customer satisfaction include:

▓ Find out what is most important to customers, for example, cost, safety, economy, reliability and so on, and then develop ways and means of finding out to what extent you are meeting those needs.

▓ Listen to what your customers have to say and take appropriate action.

▓ Never make unrealistic promises – try to manage customers' needs and expectations by, for example, advertising or negotiating a realistic specification.

▓ Make sure that promises are kept. If you say that you will ring back in the afternoon, do so.

▓ Find out how consumers perceive the quality of your products and services in relation to that of your main competitors and take appropriate action.

▓ Present customer satisfaction ratings in the form of easy-to-understand pictorial representations such as graphs or histograms (see Figure 8.1). Keep them up to date and disseminate them widely within the company.

▓ Keep a close check on brand loyalty – why do customers buy from you? Do they intend to buy from you in the future? If not, why not?

Feedback from customers can be achieved in various ways. For example:

▓ regular meetings between customers and senior management

▓ detailed market research on existing customers' needs and expectations, as well as those of potential customers

▓ surveys and questionnaires

▓ customer clinics and quality service forums which allow the company to listen to customers and take appropriate action

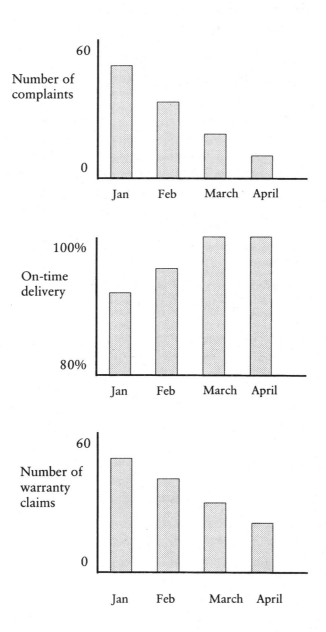

Figure 8.1 Customer satisfaction trends

▓ comment cards delivered with the service or attached to products, which the customer is encouraged to complete and which when returned are always acted upon by senior management
▓ a comprehensive analysis of all customer complaints
▓ support lines and free telephone numbers
▓ relative perceived quality surveys.

Customer complaints data should be treated with care since it is well known that only a small number of people who are actually dissatisfied bother to lodge an official complaint. Nevertheless, measuring customer satisfaction can indicate trends which make it easy for managers and employees to see whether or not things are getting better or worse. Satisfaction measures should concentrate, therefore, on trends (see Figure 8.1) and the company's position relative to its competitors – where are we in the perceived relative quality pecking order?

Performance Improvement Criteria
Customer Satisfaction

For completion by marketing/sales staff

Appraisal criteria	Appraisal rating Maximum rating = Strongly agree 1 = Strongly disagree/don't know
▓ Yardsticks for measuring customer satisfaction have been identified – for example, quality, delivery, after-sales service.	5 4 3 2 1
▓ The yardsticks are based on measures that are important to our customers.	5 4 3 2 1
▓ Customer satisfaction is measured on a regular basis.	5 4 3 2 1
▓ Pictorial representations are used to plot customer satisfaction trends for each yardstick.	5 4 3 2 1

▨ Customer satisfaction measures are
used to promote a process of
continuous improvement.   5 4 3 2 1

▨ We measure how customers perceive
our performance in relation to that of
our main competitors on a range of
key performance measures.   5 4 3 2 1

▨ We use perceived relative quality results
for benchmarking and to improve the
quality of our products and services.   5 4 3 2 1

▨ There is a system for regularly reviewing:
  – the criteria (yardsticks), used to
    measure customers' satisfaction   5 4 3 2 1
  – the way the information is gathered   5 4 3 2 1
  – how the information is analysed and
    interpreted   5 4 3 2 1
  – how the results are used.   5 4 3 2 1

▨ We have identified all external customer
contact points.   5 4 3 2 1

▨ All persons in direct contact with
customers get regular feedback on their
performance.   5 4 3 2 1

▨ There is a means of ensuring that every
customer has a clear and easy route to
register a complaint or seek advice.   5 4 3 2 1

▨ All customer complaints are dealt with
quickly and effectively.   5 4 3 2 1

▨ We ensure that all employees are aware of
feedback from customers.   5 4 3 2 1

▓ We provide customer service skills and
product knowledge training for all
relevant employees.   **5 4 3 2 1**

▓ We regularly review our product support
information and users' manuals for style,
clarity and simplicity.   **5 4 3 2 1**

Interpretation of results

80 to 90	Customer satisfaction procedures and systems are on a par with the best of the competition.
65 to 79	Significant development need.
Less than 65	Major development need.

9

Employee satisfaction

Performance measure '8'

Employees express a high degree of satisfaction with the way they are managed, developed and their skills used.

EMPLOYEE SATISFACTION

How many managers would be content with less than a full return on the assets of the business? People are an asset too, arguably the most valuable one, even though they do not appear in the company books. Consider the following statements about people and ask yourself if the same can be said of your other assets:

- People are an asset which appreciates in value over time.
- People can adapt to change in technology, work methods and the environment.
- People are flexible and can be re-trained and re-deployed.
- People are intelligent and can make decisions.
- People cannot be fully owned, easily dismissed, or disposed of as you think fit.
- People can leave you at any time.

It clearly makes sense to capitalize on these attributes. Unfortunately, most 'Mac' managers pay lip service to the need for training and developing their people, but in practice fail to exploit their creative talents and experience. As one redundant employee said: 'I guess I was laid off because our products were not good enough and yet never in twenty years did my bosses ask me how I could do my job better.' Front-line workers know the job best, know what the problems are and often know how best to solve them, but how often do management ask for their advice? Satisfied employees are more likely to cooperate in the never-ending quest for excellence than are employees who dislike their jobs, their managers and the organization itself.

If managers were judged by what they do rather than what they say, it would be fair to conclude that many of them regard their employees as people who can't be trusted to do the job themselves without close supervision. 'Mac' managers believe in tight control and telling people what to do. Empowering people to solve problems and manage themselves comes very low down on their list of priorities. Such an attitude is hardly likely to promote a process of continuous improvement or loyalty to the company. The problem is not confined, however, to non-managerial levels. A 1994 survey by the Ashridge Management College found that managers often put in 60-hour weeks and took work home, but that employers were not recognizing their efforts. As a result, half of those questioned felt less loyal to their company than they did five years ago and just one in seven said they were working for the ideal organization.

In the past, a valid measure of employees' satisfaction was given by labour turnover, but this may no longer be the case. The reasons why people leave can be complex. It is possible to anticipate certain losses for domestic reasons, but how many staff leave for other reasons, and can the company influence them? To answer these questions, it is important to ensure that leavers are interviewed to establish why they are leaving. Such an interview needs to be skilfully planned and carried out and the information obtained treated with caution. This is because employees are often reluctant to give reasons that are critical of the employer and the reasons they give are not always the real ones. Also there may be several reasons, only one of which is mentioned. The benefits of conducting an analysis of leavers by reason are:

▨ The reasons people give for leaving often have internal consistency, year by year, and so have predictive value.

▓ It becomes possible to relate particular features of leaving, for example, pregnancy to age structure.

▓ The information can be fed back to the selection process to create 'profiles' of leavers.

▓ The company may be able to see its staff relationships, often the subject of myths, in a more realistic manner.

Analysis of leavers' information may help the company answer a number of important questions. For example:

▓ Is the selection process working properly?

▓ Are training and development arrangements as good as our main competitors?

▓ Are the jobs sufficiently interesting and challenging?

▓ Has the company got a good reputation locally for the way it treats its people?

▓ Are conditions of service on a par with the best of the competition?

▓ What effect does poor management ('Mac' managers) have on turnover?

Absenteeism used to be a problem in many companies and was often a symptom of employees' dissatisfaction. However, as manning levels fall and tiers of management disappear, people are having to assume greater responsibility, take on extra work and work much longer hours. It is hardly surprising that under the pressure of longer hours, a smaller workforce, the threat of redundancy and unreasonable 'Mac' managers, that people are afraid to 'lose time', even at the risk of disrupting their family life and adversely affecting their health. In many cases, we now have an inverse relationship between absenteeism and dissatisfaction. That is, a very low absenteeism figure, especially when combined with longer working hours, might be a more reliable indicator of dissatisfaction at work than is high absenteeism. Many people are afraid to lose time for fear of losing their jobs and are 'motivated' to work longer hours by the culture of the organization. Absenteeism figures should, therefore, be treated with caution. We can no longer assume that low levels of absenteeism indicate employee satisfaction.

Actions that companies can take to promote employee satisfaction have already been discussed in Chapters 4 and 5. Other measures designed to satisfy employees' needs and retain skilled people are well illustrated by the following example. Texaco is one of 14 employers nominated for a Parents At Work award after introducing a range of flexible working options in 1993. According to a report in the *Daily Mail* (23 February 1995) Jennifer Malone, Texaco's manager of equal opportunities, is reported as saying: 'If you have invested in people, it makes good business sense to keep their skills and not lose them because they have a family or their parents are sick.' These awards are sponsored by Reed Personnel and supported by the magazine, People Management. Texaco are reacting in a positive manner to the increasing problems of reconciling the growing conflict between work commitments and family loyalties by introducing job-sharing, part-time work, up to ten weeks' extra unpaid leave during school holidays and will phase in mothers' return to work over a period of up to a year. Other companies shortlisted for the award include: Sainsbury's, Littlewoods, the regional electricity company Manweb, Portsmouth City Council, the Welsh television company S4C, the Royal Liverpool Philharmonic Society and the Scottish Council for Single Parents. In March 1995, North British Housing were declared winners of the award.

Another characteristic of WCOs is the action they take to ensure that their employees' efforts are recognized and rewarded. For example, Hills Industries (see case example in Chapter 3) have a bonus scheme in which all staff receive the same monetary benefit regardless of job position. However, bonus schemes can also be counter-productive, especially when employees have no control over some of the factors taken into consideration for the making of bonus awards. This can act as a disincentive when people have struggled hard to achieve targets only to be penalized for events outside their control. To be effective, bonus schemes must be seen to be fair and based on factors that people can influence and exercise some control over.

The most effective way of gathering valid information from employees about issues of concern to them is to ask them to complete questionnaires that cannot be traced back to the respondents. This helps to ensure that the answers are honest and hence more valid. The results can then be used by senior management to identify problem areas and decide what action to take. In WCOs employees consistently express a high degree of satisfaction with the way they are managed, trained and developed. So how does your company compare with current best practice? Use the employees' satisfaction survey shown below and find out.

Performance Improvement Criteria
Employees' Satisfaction Survey

For completion by non-supervisory employees

Appraisal criteria	Appraisal rating
	5 = Fully satisfied
	1 = Extremely dissatisfied/ don't know or doesn't apply

■ Are you satisfied with:
- senior management's commitment to training and development? **5 4 3 2 1**
- the way you are managed and supervised? **5 4 3 2 1**
- the way your skills are used? **5 4 3 2 1**
- communications within the organization? **5 4 3 2 1**
- the way your performance is appraised and the results acted upon? **5 4 3 2 1**
- the credit and praise you get for good performance or ideas? **5 4 3 2 1**
- the advice and support you get from your manager when things go wrong? **5 4 3 2 1**
- the way the company's rules and regulations are enforced? **5 4 3 2 1**
- the information you are given about the company's business performance? **5 4 3 2 1**
- the information you are given about how well the company is doing in relation to its major competitors? **5 4 3 2 1**
- the way industrial relations matters are dealt with? **5 4 3 2 1**

- the encouragement everyone is given
to seek and come forward with ideas for
improving performance?   **5 4 3 2 1**

▩ Are you satisfied with the quality of the
training you were given:
- on joining the company?   **5 4 3 2 1**
- for your first job?   **5 4 3 2 1**
- for change of job, method, procedure and
so on?   **5 4 3 2 1**

▩ Are you satisfied with the encouragement
and support the company gives you to
learn new skills or gain an appropriate
qualification?   **5 4 3 2 1**

▩ Are you satisfied with the way
management make decisions and
introduce change?   **5 4 3 2 1**

On completion of the survey an average score should be allocated to each question and a summary of the results presented to senior management for analysis and evaluation. You should cross-refer the results with Fig. 4.1 and the performance improvement criteria at the end of Chapter 5.

Interpretation of results

68 to 85   Employees express a high degree of satisfaction.

55 to 67   Significant development need.

less than 67   Major development need.

10

Community satisfaction

ETHICAL LEADERSHIP

Ethical leaders set high standards of ethical behaviour and integrity. They admit their errors when things go wrong and act promptly to put things right.

There is little point in having a code of ethics if senior management are not prepared to abide by the code themselves. The attitudes and values of employees generally are greatly influenced by the attitudes and behaviour of senior management. If the actions of managers are perceived to be fair and consistent their people will respect them, even if they don't like their management style. People like to know where they stand and managers who send out conflicting messages by the inconsistency of their actions are bound to lose the respect of their people. It is hardly surprising, therefore, that excessive pay rises for people at the top are perceived as an 'I'm all right Jack' attitude, especially when the very same managers exhort their people to accept wage increases in line with inflation or less. If sacrifices have to be made in the interests of the company, the burden should be shared by all.

Questions that should be addressed by all companies include:

▓ Does the company have a code of ethics which is widely disseminated and enforced at all levels?
▓ Does the company take a tough stand on ethical issues?
▓ Do senior management lead by example and show by their actions that they are committed to the company's code of ethics?
▓ Is the company's ethical stance rated highly by the community, ethical consumers and ethical investors?

Ethical leaders ensure that ethical codes and practices are implemented and take immediate corrective action when the code is breached. They communicate and cooperate with key players in the community to tackle ethical and environmental issues. Unfortunately, many companies either lack ethical codes and policies or they have them but managers do not take them seriously.

The Body Shop is a good example of an ethical company that has prospered. The company has always placed great store in communication between customers and shop staff, between staff and management and between business and the community.

The Body Shop does not commission or test any product or ingredient on animals and uses a combination of alternatives, for example: ingredients with a long history of safe usage, such as bananas or Brazil nut oil; computer models for microbiological analyses; controlled testing on carefully monitored groups of human volunteers; the use of highly technological alternatives to animal testing and further work developing scientific alternatives.

This is combined with the 'five-year rolling rule' under which the Body Shop's suppliers are required to complete a form which gives the last date of any animal testing that they have conducted on any ingredient which they supply to them. If the supplier reports an animal test on an ingredient for the cosmetics industry within the last five years or if the supplier refuses to supply the completed form, the Body Shop stops buying that ingredient from them and seeks an alternative source from a supplier who has not tested it on animals within the same period. If no supplier can be found who meets the five-year rule, and no alternative ingredient exists, the Body Shop stops making the product. This happened in 1992 when the Body Shop withdrew its Carrot Sun Milk 20+. This is a good example of ethical leadership in action and of the influence a customer (in this case the Body Shop) can exert on the practices and procedures of their suppliers.

The Body Shop's ethical stance has certainly paid off in terms of business success. Shares in 1986 were valued at 50 pence. In February 1995 they were valued at 178 pence. There are now over 900 branches of the Body Shop in 42 countries.

According to Henderson Touche Remnant there is now a choice of about 400 British companies in the 'ethical universe'. According to them: 'Body Shop is probably the company working hardest towards the principles of sustainable development. It has proved that its intentions are good and it acted quickly when there was a breach of its own internal policy' (*Sunday Times*, 22 January 1995).

There is ample evidence that companies which take their social responsibility seriously are generally more profitable than those which do not. The reason is partly because these companies are more sensitive and responsive to what is happening in the world about them. Companies which ignore the growing awareness amongst the public of environmental issues, do so at their peril.

ETHICAL CONSUMERS AND INVESTORS

These days millions of people invest in the stock market through unit trusts, life, pension or personal equity plans, and yet remain unsure of which companies their money is invested in. However, things are changing fast and over 20 investment fund managers now offer unit trusts, life insurance, PEPs or pension funds that invest in the stock market, but avoid areas that many people consider unethical. Many funds also engage in what is known as 'positive investment'. This entails singling out companies with the best practices in particular areas, for example, the best pollution record.

Increasingly, ethical consumers are bringing pressure to bear on companies through their purchasing power – for example, buying products perceived to be environmentally friendly. Further pressure is being exerted on companies by the growing number of ethical investors who refuse to invest in companies they consider to be unethical, for example:

▓ companies with a bad pollution record
▓ companies which sell arms
▓ companies involved in animal testing of cosmetics
▓ companies concerned with tobacco or alcohol
▓ companies that invest in countries with oppressive regimes
▓ companies involved in gambling.

ENVIRONMENTAL ISSUES

The hole in the ozone layer over the Antarctic; the storms in the UK in 1987 and 1990 which caused widespread damage to property; the threat posed by rising sea levels to, for example, the Maldives and worldwide coastal areas, the dramatic increase in asthma, especially amongst young children; and the possibility of another Chernobyl-type disaster should be sufficient to worry all of us about environmental issues. Pollution, global warming and depletion of the world's natural resources are emerging as major concerns for the 1990s. Widespread use of recycling centres and increasing support for environmental causes are proof that the general public is concerned. Businesses are also having to become more environmentally aware, not just to comply with stringent environmental legislation, but to establish a 'green' image with their customers.

Companies can no longer ignore the impact they have on the community since even 'clean' office jobs can have an influence on the environment through energy waste in paper or electricity. There has been, for example, a significant increase in demand for recycled paper in recent years, especially stationery. The British Paper Company uses 100 per cent recycled waste supplied by printers, local charities and others, which they use to supply NatWest with its blotting paper, environmental leaflets and shareholder proxy cards.

Many organizations see 'green' issues as opportunities to gain a competitive edge, but not all. During the late 1970s most companies in the chemical processing industry were claiming that expenditure on pollution control was a major drain on profitability. 3M, however, proved that planning and technological innovation could combine pollution prevention with waste prevention into a highly profitable exercise. As a result, its plants around the world made significant savings in recovered materials and reduction in energy use.

At British Steel's Port Talbot works the Engineering Energy Department used a total quality performance (TQP) team to examine ways and means of reducing the consumption of high cost domestic water. The result has been a spectacular reduction in costs. At the start of the project water consumption was 483 litres per man per day. This has been reduced to 243 litres per man per day giving a 50 per cent reduction. For the period January 1993 to June 1994 the cost savings were £847,000. TQP teams are now firmly established at British Steel and are making a significant impact on reducing costs and energy consumption.

Reviews and audits of environmental performance can also lead to significant improvements in performance. On their own, however, they cannot provide an organization with the assurance that its performance not only meets, but will continue to meet, legislative and policy requirements. To be effective, audits need to be conducted within a structured management system, integrated with overall management activity, and need to address all aspects of desired environmental performance, for example, as outlined in BS 91/55324 – Environmental Management Systems.

INVOLVEMENT IN THE COMMUNITY

Ethical leaders take their social responsibilities seriously and encourage their management teams to become actively involved in the community – not just for the sake of it but for the benefit of both the community and the company. Management need to know how the policies of key players in the community are likely to affect them. They need to be aware of how the community perceives the company in relation to safety, ethical and environmental issues. They also need to know if the company is perceived as a good company to work for and, if not, why not. How many managers, for example, know the answers to the following questions?

- How are the policies of the local Training and Enterprise Council (TEC) likely to affect your company?
- Do you know what the aims and objectives of the TEC are?
- Do you know which of your competitors have managers serving on TEC boards?
- Does your company participate in the Understanding Industry scheme?
- How many of your managers serve on committees of relevant local bodies?
- Does your company participate in industry/education partnerships?

There are many sound reasons why companies should be involved in the local community. For example, British Steel Tinplate are actively involved in the Understanding Industry scheme which is a national education/industry partnership organization that specializes in providing 16–19 year old students with a broader awareness of industry and commerce. The scheme provides them with the opportunity to communicate with, and influence, the future managers and opinion formers of the twenty-first century.

Companies which are not actively involved in the community are missing opportunities to influence key policy-makers in their area. Involvement in the community also provides the opportunity to create an image of the company as one that cares about the welfare and wellbeing of both its own people and the community in which they live. In the end it comes down to attitude. If companies see fulfilling their social responsibilities as a necessary chore rather than an opportunity to maintain and expand their reputations and standing in the community, they are limiting their flexibility to respond to what happens in the outside world.

Performance Improvement Criteria
Impact on the Community

For completion by senior management

Appraisal criteria	Appraisal rating Maximum rating = Strongly agree 1 = Strongly disagree/don't know

Note: some of the criteria require a yes or no answer, ie 5 or 1 score

▓ The company has a written statement of its
code of ethics/social responsibilities.   **5 4 3 2 1**

▓ The code of ethics is strictly enforced
at all levels in the company.   **5 4 3 2 1**

▓ The company fully complies with
environmental legislation.   **5 4 3 2 1**

▓ The company has an environmental
management system covering:
- policy   **5 4 3 2 1**
- responsibilities and organization   **5 4 3 2 1**
- objectives/targets   **5 4 3 2 1**
- operational control   **5 4 3 2 1**
- audits   **5 4 3 2 1**
- reviews.   **5 4 3 2 1**

▓ The company is actively involved in
community activities.   **5 4 3 2 1**

▓ Surveys are occasionally carried out to
assess the company's impact on the
community in respect of:
- environmental issues   **5 4 3 2 1**
- health and safety   **5 4 3 2 1**
- sponsorship and involvement in the
community   **5 4 3 2 1**

- the company's image on caring and
  ethical issues. **5 4 3 2 1**

▓ The company's performance is on a
par with the best of the competition
in respect of:
- health and safety matters **5 4 3 2 1**
- environmental issues **5 4 3 2 1**
- involvement in the community **5 4 3 2 1**
- image as a caring and ethical company. **5 4 3 2 1**

▓ The company regularly reviews its
policy and impact on the local community. **5 4 3 2 1**

▓ Companies have been identified that
could be used for benchmarking purposes. **5 4 3 2 1**

Interpretation of results

85 to 100   Safety, environmental and ethical practices are on a par
with the best of the competition.

75 to 84   Significant development need.

Less than 75   Major development need.

11

Investor satisfaction

Performance measure '10'

Investors express satisfaction with the company's business
results which are as good as, or better than, the best of the
competition.

BUSINESS RESULTS

At the business level, customers (markets) and shareholders determine
what it is important to measure and the competition determines how
good your performance is. Unfortunately it is often difficult to look at
a profit and loss account or balance sheet and get a full picture. To
overcome this problem ratios are often used to interpret business
performance. A ratio is simply a relationship between two numbers. It
indicates how a business is performing and can show trends and patterns when compared to the same ratios for previous years and to those
of similar businesses. One of the advantages of financial ratios is that
they enable companies to compare their performance with that of their
main competitors. A detailed explanation of financial ratios is outside
the scope of this book, but some of the more important are:

1.   Gross profit margin = Gross profit × 100/sales

The gross profit margin can be used to compare your own performance against that of other companies. It can also be used to compare a company's performance over time.

2.　　　　　Net profit margin = Profit before tax × 100/sales

The net profit margin gives you the picture after taking off your overheads and interest before tax. An increasing figure shows good control of overheads and vice versa.

3.
$$\text{Return on capital} = \frac{\text{Profit before charging interest on tax} \times 100}{\text{Total capital employed}}$$

The return on capital ratio measures how productive your business is. **This is one of the most important ratios** since it tells investors how well their money is performing. The return on investment should be at least equal to the return investors could get if they invested in a building society, bank or national savings.

4.
$$\text{Earnings per share} = \frac{\text{After - tax profits}}{\text{Number of ordinary shares issued}}$$

Investors naturally look for an upward trend. Profits retained for investment in the company should help to ensure that profits continue to increase in the future.

5.
$$\text{Price earnings p / e} = \frac{\text{Market price of an ordinary share}}{\text{Earnings per share}}$$

The higher the ratio is, the more confident investors are likely to be that future profits are going to be higher or that shares are going to be worth more in the future. The lower the p/e ratio the more concerned investors are likely to be about future returns on their investment.

6.

$$\text{Dividend yield} = \frac{\text{Dividend per share}}{\text{Market price per share}} \times 100$$

The dividend yield is a measure of the return received in cash on the money invested, and is based on the value of the investment as being the present market price at which the share may be purchased or sold. Investors naturally look for an upward trend.

In recent years, some companies, especially in the United States, have introduced performance measures related to the creation of shareholder value. One of these is known as Market Value Added (MVA). MVA shows whether a company has made or lost money for its shareholders. It gives a verdict on performance stretching back for some years.

The idea of MVA is simple. It takes the total capital that is available, adding up the money raised through share issues, borrowings and retained earnings, to give a simple measure of how much money investors have poured into a company. It then takes the current value of the company's shares and debt as a measure of what investors could take out of the company. The difference between the two is the MVA, which measures how executives have managed the capital at their disposal. A positive MVA indicates that value has increased, whereas a negative MVA indicates that value has declined. In this way, it is possible to rank companies in order of their MVA. It also shows whether a company's performance has improved over time by comparing the MVA, for example, in 1995 with that of 1997.

MVA shows whether a company is making or losing shareholder value but it does not predict whether a company is going to improve or decline. For this purpose, a measure known as Economic Value Added (EVA) is used. This measure takes a company's after-tax operating profit and compares it with its cost of capital. The cost of capital includes the cost of equity – what shareholders have an expectation of receiving through capital gains and dividends – as well as the cost of bonds and bank loans.

The EVA figures represent the difference between profit and the cost of capital. The assumption is that it is not good enough for a company to simply make profit; it has to make enough to justify the cost of its capital, including equity. If it is not covering that it will not make good returns for investors. Most measures of performance, such as earnings per share, ignore the cost of capital in a business. Despite its critics, there does appear to be a close correlation between a positive EVA and long-term MVA growth.

One benefit from using the MVA/EVA measures of performance is to force managers to realize that their main objective is to make a return on the money in the business. For example, many managers are paid a bonus based on sales which often encourages them to order excessive stock because if they are not able to sell it at full price, they know that they could sell it in a sale, which is good for turnover, and hence bonuses, but bad for profits.

Ultimately, the main reason for introducing EVA is to increase its MVA. Common sense suggests that so long as a company keeps earning more than the cost of its capital, it should result in a rising share price which should lead to a rising MVA.

The EVA/MVA concept of measurement is certainly worth considering but there are problems. For example,

- If a company is investing large sums of money in research and development, its EVA may be negative, even though it may pay rich dividends in years to come.
- MVA is an historical measure of performance rather than an indicator of future success.
- MVA is greatly influenced by the share price at the time of the snapshot.
- It is difficult to demonstrate a link between EVA and the current market valuations of companies.
- No one performance measure can hope to capture the full picture.

The dangers of relying on a single measure can be illustrated by the case of British Gas. According to the rankings produced by Stern Steward based on the EVA/MVA concept, British Gas occupied 22nd place in the rankings in 1995, but had fallen dramatically to 468th place in 1996. EVA/MVA measures failed to predict such a disastrous result. However, using the ten Performance Measures of Business Success outlined in this book would have shown that all was not well at British Gas in 1995, despite its 22nd place in the MVA/EVA rankings. At that time customer, employee and investor satisfaction levels were at an all time low. The management style of the company, especially at senior levels, also came in for much criticism – much of which was unfair since the company was going through a period of dramatic change. Nevertheless, using the ten PMs, the company would have been rated very low – a score of 1 or 2 at the most – on at least four of the ten performance measures.

Despite these caveats, companies should, nevertheless, explore the MVA/EVA system in detail to help them decide whether they should introduce the concept in conjunction with existing performance measures. To focus only on shareholder value added would be a mistake since a company depends for its success on satisfied customers, competent and motivated employees, and leaders with vision who can create the conditions and ethos needed to compete effectively in a rapidly changing world where past success is no guarantee of future success.

Performance Improvement Criteria
Business Results

For completion by senior management

Appraisal criteria	Appraisal rating 10 = Appraisal criterion fully met 1 = Appraisal criterion not met at all

▓ We have established procedures
for measuring market performance,
for example: **10 7 5 3 1**

  – Absolute market share
  – Relative market share
  – Market share rank.

▓ We have established procedures for
measuring our financial performance,
for example: 10 7 5 3 1

   – Gross profit margin
   – Net profit margin
   – Return on capital
   – Earnings per share
   – Price earnings
   – Dividend yield
   – Market value added (MVA)
   – Economic value added (EVA).

▓ We have effective systems for
establishing:

   – How satisfied investors are with
     our business results   10 7 5 3 1
   – How our business results compare
     with the best of the competition.   10 7 5 3 1

▓ We regularly review and update our
market and financial measures with a
view to improving:

   – The relevance of the measures   10 7 5 3 1
   – The collection of information   10 7 5 3 1
   – Analysis of the results   10 7 5 3 1
   – Presentation of information   10 7 5 3 1
   – Dissemination of information.   10 7 5 3 1

▓ We have identified organizations
that we could use for benchmarking
purposes.   10 7 5 3 1

Interpretation of results

90 to 100   Market and financial measures and information systems
                 on a par with the best of the competition.

80 to 89   Significant development need.

Less than 80   Major development need.

12

The management of change

A customer and stakeholder strategy based on benchmarking and investment in people and technology pays.

British firms are beginning to respond to the realities of the worldwide competitive battle and many of them emerged from the recession fitter and leaner. According to a report by the broker Société Générale Strauss Turnbull, which focused on 31 of the biggest British companies, Britain has narrowed the productivity (output per employee) gap with Germany and for a brief period in 1992 actually overtook the Germans. In the case of British Steel, for example, there has been an incredible fourfold increase in productivity since the end of the 1970s, as is illustrated by the following case example:

The emergence of British Steel plc, which before privatization in 1988 was known as the British Steel Corporation (BSC), as one of the top steelmakers in the world represents a remarkable British success story.

Today British Steel is the fourth largest steelmaker in the world and is one of Britains's leading exporters, with overseas sales accounting for nearly half of the 1993/4 £4.3 billion turnover.

The company's aim is to continue to be a major force in the world steel industry by providing the best steel products, produced in the most efficient manner and delivered to the customer in a way that gives those customers the most value.

By the end of 1980, the British Steel Corporation (BSC) had completed the closure of a number of out-dated loss-making plants and reduced its workforce to 130,000 compared with a total of 268,500 employees at the time of nationalization in 1967. This reduction was accompanied by a massive programme of guidance and re-training of redundant employees, including the establishment of British Steel (Industry), a company whose role was to attract new investment in areas where redundancies were to be made and to advise employees on how to set up in business on their own account. This drive to reduce the steel cost base has continued and for 1993/4 the average number of employees was 41,300.

In 1980 BSC introduced the principle of locally negotiated bonus schemes through which employees could earn more in exchange for an agreement on more efficient working practices, reduced manning levels and commitment to quality and related training. Largely self-financing, this approach to the pay structure resulted in substantial improvements in overall earnings levels throughout the Corporation, and was an important factor in BSC's recovery to profitability.

A further major element in the reduction of the cost base has been the continuing capital investment programme which the company has maintained over several years. Major schemes such as the switch to 100 per cent continuous casting, upgrading of hot strip mills, a new galvanizing line, continuous cold rolling facilities, improvement to paint-coating plants, etc. have produced improvements in yield, more consistent product quality and reduced energy consumption.

By early 1984, the Corporation was achieving better labour productivity levels than most continental steelmakers and, since privatization, this trend has been continued by British Steel plc, so that in 1993/4 a figure of 3.8 man hours per tonne was recorded – a fourfold improvement since the end of the 1970s.

The turnaround in British Steel's fortunes since the early years of the 1980s has been dramatic. In November 1994, Brian Moffat, chairman and chief executive, announced that half-year pre-tax profits were up from £27 million in 1993/4 to £159 million in 1994/5 for the six months to 1 October. Additionally, British Steel is the lowest cost producer in Europe.

British Steel's turnaround is all the more remarkable when taking into account the unfair competition from subsidized overseas competitors and the over capacity in the European Union of around 30 million tonnes which depress prices, reduce utilization rates and thereby increase costs and reduce margins. European governments, by their protective attitudes, condone over-production in an industry that is not generating proper profit margins.

Many experts predict that having weathered the recession of the early 1990s, British Steel's pre-tax profits will surge towards £400 million in 1994–5, up from £80 million in 1993–4. These results, coupled with shrewd and timely strategic moves and acquisitions, for example, a £97 million investment in British Steel's Tuscaloosa mini-mill in Alabama, an £85 million purchase of an additional 9.9 per cent stake in its stainless-steel joint venture with Sweden's Avesta, and a triple alliance with LTV of America and Japan's Sumitomo Metal Industries to build a £274 million mini-mill in America, are likely to reinforce British Steel's position as a world class quality organization.

Apart from measures to improve efficiency and profitability, British Steel's remarkable turnaround has been based on a number of key elements. These include continuous improvement of quality, close coop-eration with customers and suppliers, pollution control, energy conser-vation and training to achieve business objectives. For example, in 1992 the British Steel strip products (BSSP), one of British Steel's flat products businesses, established multi-disciplined task teams to focus resources on achievement of a series of ambitious targets relating to quality, consistency, yields, delivery performance, etc. The methodology used was based on successful Japanese practices and task team members spent some time in Japan to see the Japanese approach to focused problem solving being put into operation. The results of this initiative were so good that the practice has been expanded into many areas of business activities.

Major benefits have also been achieved from the application of statistical process control techniques, and research efforts focused on meeting the increasing quality and technical demands from customers, establishing new uses for steel and competing with alternative materials. The overall objective of the quality improvement process has been to focus on the quality necessary to achieve the key requirements of customer service and internal efficiency in line with best world standards.

As part of the drive to improve customer service, advisory engineers who are based in the regions of the UK market and in each of the major European markets, including Scandinavia, Germany, Benelux, France and Iberia, are equipped with a travelling office in the shape of a briefcase housing a powerful laptop PC, a small printer, a hand portable cellphone together with integral power supplies and circuitry. The aim is to speed up the handling of customer complaints and to be more responsive to customer problems. The advisory engineer is able to have immediate contact by telephone directly to any BSSP location; send and receive faxes to and from anywhere; and have on-line access to the Port Talbot mainframe computer from any point within the UK. Advisory engineers are no longer dependent on making regular detours to sales offices to contact base, receive messages or deal with queries. Customer complaints can be dealt with on the spot with the customer, and reports sent directly to the supplying works using the fax link.

British Steel works closely with all its customers. For example the Shotton works received a special supplier commendation from Nissan (customer) in May 1994, for improvement in quality and customer service. This was quickly followed by the prestigious Q1 quality award from the Ford Motor company which was achieved through a close working relationship with Ford, one of their major customers. Similarly, British Steel (customer) works closely with its suppliers and helps them to achieve process control, consistent quality and on-time delivery. Continuous improvement and cooperation with customers and suppliers are key elements in British Steel's drive to achieve world class standards in all aspects of the business.

British Steel's commitment to tackling environmental issues is demonstrated by its involvement with the National Rivers Authority (NRA) in the launch of a promotional package 'Pollution Prevention Pays' at the Ebbw Vale works. It was British Steel's commitment to the protection of the local environment that prompted the NRA to consider using Ebbw Vale to launch their awareness programme. Another example of British Steel's active involvement in the community is the Dyfed/British Steel Tinplate technology initiative launched in 1990 to support teachers in the development of technology in the National Curriculum.

Training at all levels designed to achieve business objectives has underpinned British Steel's drive to improve quality, customer service and efficiency. For this purpose, standards of performance for each of the many hundreds of jobs have been identified by line managers supported

> by training and personnel staff. Internal committees identify and up-date core competencies for each function and each works can adapt aspects of the standards to its own needs. The standards are used for training and assessment purposes and to evaluate the effectiveness of training provision.
>
> British Steel's commitment to continuous improvement of all aspects of the business operation to achieve world class standards of customer service and internal efficiency has been a key factor in making British Steel a low-cost, high quality, profitable and internationally respected steel producer.

WCOs are not, of course, immune from recession, competition at home and abroad, or from having to compete against subsidized competitors. They tend, however, to suffer less than the competition by responding more quickly and effectively to external changes and thus holding their relative market position and profitability.

A customer focus based on benchmarking and investment in people and technology to improve efficiency and effectiveness pays. This is confirmed by the success of customer-centred organizations worldwide and is certainly true of five companies featured in this book as case examples. These are:

British Steel	Fourfold increase in productivity. Lowest cost steel producer in Europe.
Monsanto Newport Plant	Productivity rising by 67 per cent over the past five years; meeting tough production, quality and environmental standards with fewer staff.
The Whitbread Beer Company, Magor	Productivity gains of 25 per cent; meeting ambitious quality targets.
Hills Industries	In the last five years turnover has doubled and market share increased from 22 per cent to 36 per cent to become the UK market leader.

The Body Shop   Shares up from 50 pence in 1986 to 178
                                 pence in 1995. Expanded to over 400
                                 branches in 42 countries.

In the future, ethical and environmental issues are likely to be significant factors leading to business success. The Body Shop has demonstrated how effective ethical leadership, when combined with ethical
policies which are strictly enforced, can be. Clearly, companies can no
longer ignore the concerns and perceptions of the community at large.
The climate within which companies operate is clearly at a turning
point.

For many so-called knowhow companies, retention of key people,
that is, people whose loss would have a significant impact on the
companies' performance and who would be difficult to replace, is an
important factor in maintaining investors' confidence, especially as
more and more companies evolve into so-called knowhow companies
which are critically dependent on the skills and knowledge of their
employees. Another key factor in business success is investment in
people which should be sufficient to ensure that there is an adequate
supply of skilled people to meet operational demands and contingencies at all levels within the organization.

The importance of investment in capital and research and development depends on the type and size of business operation. What is
important, however, is that investment is on a par with the best of the
competition because it is difficult to counter a competitor's cost advantage based on investment in technology by cutting costs. In addition to
investment, many companies have discovered to their cost that success
in the marketplace depends on concentration of resources on a few key
products or services and getting the timing of the launch right. Many
products and services fail because they are launched at the wrong time.
This is known as the ICT strategy, that is, innovation, concentration
and timing.

A particular worry for European companies is the differential between their unit labour costs (a combination of wage costs and productivity to give a statistic for total efficiency) and those of some of their
major overseas competitors, particularly the USA and companies in
the Pacific basin. Increasingly, major companies are relocating to

low-wage countries where they are able to maximize profits at the expense of labour – for example, global free trade and competitive pressures have effectively reduced real wages in America by 15 per cent in the last 20 years.

As Japan continues to improve its legendary productivity and develop innovative high-tech products, the threat to Europe is likely to be particularly acute as the European Union tries to remain competitive, whilst, at the same time, trying to constrain the spiralling cost of its social policies. Already, serious clashes have taken place between Britain and its European partners on the issue of the minimum wage, which Britain argues, rightly or wrongly, destroys jobs. The truth is, however, that Britain relies on low wages to attract inward investment and to compensate for its low productivity in relation to its main competitors.

Although wages in the British motor industry in 1992 were lower than those in America, Japan and all mainland European countries, productivity was so poor that unit labour costs in Britain were higher than anywhere else. This surprising fact was reported by the VDA, Germany's equivalent of the Society of Motor Manufacturers and Traders. Things are improving, however, and Ford reported early in 1994 that unit costs in its British plants were lower than its German factories, although still higher than in Belgium and Spain. A survey of 71 plants in nine countries by 'Anderson Consulting' of car component suppliers, showed that although British plants made substantial productivity improvements between 1992 and 1994, Britain still came out bottom in Europe for productivity and second lowest for quality. The report says that Japanese car makers 'have shown that high performance is possible in the UK. The problem we face is that it is just not travelling down the supply chain fast enough'.

FUTURE WORK PATTERNS AND PRACTICES

Although prediction is a hazardous business, it is possible to discern future work patterns and practices from a consideration of the characteristics and practices of the emerging customer-centred organization described in this book. For example:

▓ As companies become 'flatter and leaner', there is likely to be an increase in outsourcing and the use of part-time workers and consultants.

▓ There is likely to be a marked increase in joint projects and other activities involving customers, suppliers and key players in the community working on topics and issues of common interest – for example, design and development of customized products and services, environmental issues, industry/education partnerships and quality assurance.

▓ As more companies recognize the true cost of losing their key people, there is likely to be an expansion of flexible working arrangements designed to help people cope with the growing conflict between work and family commitments.

▓ There is likely to be greater emphasis on 'people flexibility' and less on job descriptions – people will be expected to do any task which they are competent to perform and take more responsibility for continuously up-dating their skills and knowledge.

▓ Project-based management is likely to increase and the consultative and delegation leadership styles predominate – in unstructured situations there are no experts. People will leave and enter projects as skill requirements change.

▓ There is likely to be a marked increase in self-employed people working from home who will assume responsibility for their own self-development and management – for example, investing in their own development, negotiating contracts, accessing information (Internet and e-mail) and marketing themselves and their services to prospective customers and clients.

▓ The computer will empower people by giving them greater access to information. For example, Internet and e-mail will enable individuals to gather information from around the world. Electronic mail enables more people to participate in the decision-making process and is, therefore, more likely to generate quality decisions than would be the case, for example, at a meeting where a small vocal minority often dominate proceedings. E-mail enables a person to quickly call upon the expertise of a great many people, – thus maximizing the chances of generating a quality decision or original solution to a problem.

▓ Education and training is likely to become more integrated with greater emphasis on core, vocational, technical and business skills. Industry/education partnerships are likely to increase and universities devote more time to creating and developing innovative products and services in partnership with companies. Euroqualifications which seek to establish a common approach to vocational qualifications are likely to be established within the European Union. The information 'superhighway' and virtual reality are likely to revolutionize education and training practices.

▓ There is likely to be an increase in the sharing of information on best practices amongst companies that do not compete with one another. Benchmarking all aspects of the business operation against the best of the competition worldwide is likely to become widespread.

▓ There is likely to be a big increase in computer networking within and between companies, thus making it possible to separate tasks geographically and still maintain centralized control. Similarly, workflow computing which automates the flow of information to support the flow of work is also likely to increase sharply.

▓ 'Mobile workers', armed with mobile phone, laptop computer and fax, will be able to operate from virtually anywhere in the world and deal with customers' needs and complaints on the spot. Linked to a company's central computer, it will be possible for them to significantly reduce customer response times.

▓ There is likely to be an explosive increase in home-based shopping and banking, combined with an increase in cashless transactions. This will inevitably lead to major reductions in manpower.

▓ There is likely to be a huge increase in data base marketing and the use of customer profiles to target groups and individuals – customization, service and value for money will be at the heart of the competitive battle.

PERFORMANCE PROFILE

When you have completed the appraisal of your performance using the ten performance measures – pages 7 and 8 – you should construct a performance profile such as that shown in Figure 12.1. The profile can be used to:

- give an at-a-glance view of the company's current position in relation to the best of the competition for each of the performance measures
- decide priorities and agree an action plan
- allocate resources
- monitor and record progress in managing the change needed to become a world class player.

The action plan will, of course, concentrate on identifying the causes of poor performance highlighted by the profile. For this purpose the performance improvement criteria (PICs) contained in Chapters 2 to 11, which underpin each of the performance measures, can be used. This diagnostic process can be done by individuals or performance improvement teams.

The PICs are not cast in concrete or comprehensive and it is for each company to decide what changes to make to them before beginning the diagnostic process. As practices, procedures and standards change so the PICs will need to change as well.

Whatever the outcome of the diagnostic process, each company will have to go through a step-by-step process of improvement covering the following stages which are briefly summarized here:

1. Foster customer-centred leadership

Senior managers should make a commitment to become a world class organization and disseminate the information to all levels within the organization. They should ensure that resources and investment in people and technology are adequate to achieve world class standards of performance, customer satisfaction and business results. They should provide the leadership necessary to become a world class player by giving their people a clear vision of where the company is going, and leading by example.

2. Develop a customer-centred strategy

A customer/stakeholder strategy based on benchmarking and investment in people and technology pays. The company's mission, business objectives and policies should be spread throughout the organization and individuals held responsible for ensuring that policy is adhered to from the top down to the shopfloor. In particular, the company should promote partnerships with key players and close cooperation with customers, suppliers and the community in the design, improvement and customization of products and services.

3. Cultivate customer-centred management

Managers should critically examine the way people are managed and encourage them to be actively involved in the decision-making process. This is growing in importance because workforces are becoming better educated, technology is changing rapidly and work patterns are becoming more unstructured. In these situations, the more brainpower that can be brought to bear on problems, the better the chance of generating high quality solutions. Hence the need to empower and train individuals and teams to pool their ideas, tackle problems together and, on occasions, manage themselves.

4. Invest in people

The aim should be to have a sufficient supply of competent people at all levels within the organization to cope with current demands, change and contingencies. Training should be customized to meet specific needs, and should be competence based and cost effective. Training aimed at improving team work and flexibility should be a high priority for any company wanting to become a world class player. Without motivated, competent and adaptable people, no company can hope to remain in the top league for long, this is especially true for the growing numbers of 'knowhow' organizations.

5. Improve resource management

Customer satisfaction, productivity and flexibility are instrumental in winning competitive battles. Greater emphasis is currently being given to improving flexibility, for example lead times, on-time delivery, the sharing of common processes, and reducing the time from concept to market. A company's ability to respond quickly to changing circumstances depends on its investment and effective use of technology and the competence and adaptability of its people. Close cooperation and partnerships with customers and suppliers is another important factor, especially if processes are to be brought under control and 'just-in-time' delivery systems established.

6. Improve process control

Failing to satisfy customer needs first time costs the average company between 15 and 30 per cent of sales revenue, increasing to 40 per cent for the average service organization. Many of these losses are due to costly processing mistakes. It is important, therefore, to identify internal and external customers, find out what their needs are and then establish relevant performance measures and immediate feedback systems that let you know when things go wrong. If a process works well, try to improve it – if it doesn't work well, re-engineer it. Identify the best companies with which to compare your performance.

7. Pursue customer satisfaction

Satisfied and loyal customers are a major factor in the long-term success of an organization and in building a strong foundation for a positive company image. Customer satisfaction means identifying what is important to the customer – cost, safety, reliability, etc – and finding out ways to measure how well you are meeting those needs and, very importantly, how well you are doing in relation to your main competitors. In other words, how do customers perceive your products and services in relation to your main competitors? You should listen to your customers and take appropriate action, but never make a promise you cannot keep.

8. Motivate employees and assess their satisfaction

Leavers with an intimate knowledge of the company's policies, procedures and systems are difficult and costly to replace. If key people are leaving, check your recruitment and testing procedures for validity and reliability, check on management style, especially the degree of supervision exercised, examine ways and means of making jobs more interesting and challenging and of giving people greater control over their work, including making decisions and solving problems themselves. Importantly, give them the opportunity to satisfy their need for personal development and promotion within the organization. Employees' efforts should be recognized and rewarded by ensuring that salaries and profit-related pay are competitive. Finally, devise a means of finding out what employees feel about the way they are managed and trained and how their skills are put to use, and act on the information.

9. Monitor community satisfaction

There is increasing concern about pollution, safety and ethical issues, as is shown by the increasing number of ethical investors, and no company can hope to become a truly world class player unless account is taken of community concerns. Senior management should lead by example and ensure that there is a code of ethics which is spread throughout the organization and is strictly enforced. Active participation in the local community should be encouraged and community concerns taken into account when developing new products and services. An attempt should be made to find out how the company is perceived by the local community and the community at large, in order to take positive action on issues of concern and to develop the right company image.

10. Satisfy investors

Investor satisfaction depends, of course, on the performance and business results of the company, which in the case of a world class organization (as defined in this book) should be as good as, or better than, the best of the competition. Investors look for good returns on their money, and positive and growing market value added. However, like people, companies go through good and bad times, and it is important to explain to investors the reasons for good and bad performance, especially in companies engaged in research and development, who may not show an immediate return but offer good long-term prospects. Similarly, companies that export most of their goods and services can be hard hit by currency fluctuations and unfair competition from subsidized firms. The important question to ask is how well is the company doing in relation to its main competitors – it may be low down the league table in absolute terms but at the top in its own sector.

Performance profile

Performance rating:

WCO = Practices, performance and business results are as good as, or better than, the best of the competition.
SDN = Significant development need.
MDN = Major development need.

Characteristic of business success	Performance rating		
	WCO	SDN	MDN
'1' Senior management's commitment to world class standards.			
'2' Customer-centred strategy.			
'3' Management of people.			
'4' Supply of competent and flexible people at all levels.			
'5' Utilization of resources.			
'6' Productivity, flexibility and unit costs.			
'7' Customer satisfaction.			
'8' Employee satisfaction.			
'9' Community satisfaction.			
'10' Investor satisfaction.			

Figure 12.1 Customer–centred organizations' performance profile

Further reading

Bendell, Tony, John Kelly, Ted Merry and Fraser Sims, *Quality Measuring and Monitoring*, Century Business, 1993.

Department of Trade and Industry, *Total Quality Management and Effective Leadership*, October 1991.

Halse, Fiona, and John Humphrey, *Profits from Improved Productivity*, Kogan Page, 1986.

National Westminster Bank, *Making the Most of Your Business*, 1993.

Peters, Tom, *Thriving on Chaos*, Pan Books, 1987.

Sveiby, Karl Erick, and Tom Lloyd, *Managing Knowhow*, Bloomsbury, 1988.

Index